Unraveling The Holy Spirit Controversy

A Look at the Person and Work of the Holy Spirit

Dr. Larry A. Maxwell

Unraveling The Holy Spirit Controversy

A Look at the Person and Work of the Holy Spirit

by

Dr. Larry A. Maxwell

Dedicated to Dr. John R. Rice and Larry Coy. Those two men
of God taught me so many important truths about the Person
and Work of the Holy Spirit. They also exemplified the Power
of the Holy Spirit in their lives and ministries.
Also dedicated to Elwin Perry Fitch and Elwin Earl Fitch, my
father-in-law and brother-in-law. It was very obvious to all
who knew them, these two men knew God and walked with
Him in the power of His Holy Spirit.
All four of these men now walk with God in Heaven

All Bible passages used in this text are from the
Authorized King James Version.

Published by Challenge International
1130 Perry Rd., Afton, New York 13730
599 Route 311, Patterson, New York 12563
GoodInformation.US

ISBN-13: 978-1502429643
ISBN-10: 1502429640

Cover Design by Matthew Reid Maxwell
Cover Photo Used by Permission © Travis Hallmark

Table of Contents

Chapter 13   The Gifts of the Holy Spirit: The Gifts

Chapter 14   The Gifts of the Holy Spirit: The Ministries

Dr. Larry A. Maxwell

Introduction

One of the most wonderful truths I ever learned is God wants everyone to experience an abundant life. The sad thing is many people live mediocre or unfulfilled lives. To experience the fullness of life God wants for us, we need to have a personal relationship with Him and with His people.

It is easy to have a personal relationship with God. He did everything to make that possible. On the other hand, some people find it difficult to have a good relationship with God's people. God wants His people to have a wonderful relationship with each other, united in both doctrine and love. Sabine Baring-Gould, writer of the grand old hymn, *Onward Christian Soldiers*, said it well, back in 1865, when he wrote:

> *We are not divided, all one army we,*
> *One in hope and doctrine, one in charity.*

Here it is, close to 150 years later and I am saddened to say, well-meaning Christians are not united. We need to address that problem.

One major thing, which divides us, is a misunderstanding of the doctrine of the Holy Spirit. The very doctrine, which should be the basis for our unity, and which the Bible says is one we must agree on, has become a source of great controversy and division. I have seen that division among God's people for too many years.

My experience with the teaching on the Holy Spirit is very diverse. My grandparents on both sides were regular church attenders but my parents only attended church occasionally. As I was growing up, we hardly ever discussed Christian doctrine at home. Though I know my parents had a personal relationship with Jesus Christ, they never spoke to me about the importance of me having that same relationship. I am so thankful our church participated in a monthly skating fellowship with other churches. It was at one of those skating fellowship I heard the gospel and responded to an invitation to place my trust in Jesus Christ as my Personal Savior. I was eight years old at the time and knew exactly what I was doing.

I am also thankful our church had a Christian scouting program called *Boys Brigade*. Through that program, I received a good biblical foundation, which covered many aspects of Christian doctrine.

While I was in high school, the church I attended had a youth leader who got me involved in an exciting new movement called *The Jesus People*. The Jesus People was an early part of what became known as the *Charismatic Movement*. We went to enthusiastic concerts, rallies and Bible studies with Christians from many different churches. One of the focuses of that movement was the Holy Spirit.

After I graduated from High School, I moved to Connecticut, where I became involved in a *Charismatic* coffeehouse ministry in a *Nazarene Church*. It was there I *started* my training for ministry. Most people do not realize there is a difference between the *Pentecostal* and *Charismatic* teaching on the Holy Spirit. The Nazarene Church is traditionally *Pentecostal*. A denominational leader became upset when he learned that church was following a *Charismatic* view on the Holy Spirit. He made some significant changes and many of us left.

A Local Baptist Church asked me to become its Youth Pastor. The Pastor gave me on the job training. That helped me become aware of my need for further formal training. The Lord led me to continue my ministry training at *Practical Bible Training School (now called Davis College),* in Johnson City, New York. It is one of the oldest Bible Schools in America *(founded in 1900)*. I did not realize at the time, that school took a strong stand against the *Charismatic* movement. The definition the school used for *Charismatic* doctrine, at that time, was actually the definition of *Pentecostal* doctrine.

While at that school, I encountered another movement I was previously unaware of, known as *Calvinism*. Many *Calvinists* have a different view of the Holy Spirit than *Charismatics* and *Pentecostals*. I gained a lot of personal experience with *Charismatics, Pentecostals, non-Charismatics, non-Pentecostals, Calvinists* and *non-Calvinists*.

After Practical I attended *Liberty Baptist College (now called Liberty University)* in Lynchburg, Virginia. I was exposed to another biblical view on the Holy Spirit when I sat under the dynamic teaching of Larry Coy and Ed Hindson. They helped me understand the life-changing outline God gives in relationship to *Spiritual Gifts*. Years later, I was honored, when Larry Coy asked if he could use some of my materials.

While at Liberty, I met Dr. John R. Rice, one of the godliest men I have ever known. Dr. Rice became one of my mentors. I am so thankful the Lord used those men to show me a teaching on the Holy Spirit, which unites, rather than divides Christians.

If you put aside preconceived notions and approach this book with an open heart and open mind, it will help unravel the Holy Spirit Controversy for you. With that controversy unraveled, believers can unite in Jesus Christ and unlock the dynamic power of the *Three-fold Work of the Holy Spirit*.

This material was originally written for an upper level course for a Bible College. That class met for three hours of classroom instruction each week for 15 weeks. Later, these materials were expanded for use in a Seminary class. I also use these materials in seminars, Bible conferences and Sunday Schools around the world.

This book is good for personal study but is also a good text for a Sunday School Class or Small Group Study. Some of the chapters will take more time to cover than others.

May God help you unravel the Holy Spirit Controversy
and unleash His awesome power in your life!

Editorial Notes

All Biblical quotations used in this book are from the *Authorized King James Bible (KJV)*.

The Greek Text used is the *Received Greek Text*, often referred to as the *Textus Receptus*.

Words from the Biblical Hebrew and Greek texts are used throughout this book to help clarify the teaching. To make it easier to read, instead of using Greek or Hebrew typefaces, which many people could not read, English letters were substituted for each character *(transliteration)*.

If a word appears in a verse in *italics*, that is how it appears in the King James Bible. The King James translators used *italics* for words, which were not in the original texts, but which they believed help clarify the meaning of the Greek or Hebrew words.

Bold letters were not used in the verses in the King James Bible. When a word appears in a verse in **bold letters**, in this book, the **bold** is used for emphasis.

Sometimes Greek or Hebrew words are provided in parenthesis ( ) in some verses, in this book, after the English word(s) from the King James Bible.

If a word appears in brackets [ ] the words in the brackets are not in the actual verse but were added for clarification.

Many words in this book are unconventionally Capitalized, *italicized* or appear in **bold text**, for extra ***Emphasis***.

CHAPTER ONE

Controversy Over the Holy Spirit

What is Pneumatology?

It is very important to understand, people with very different beliefs about the Holy Spirit often use the same words but do not mean the same thing.

It is similar to the way people use the word *dinner*. People use the word, *dinner*, to mean different things. What comes to your mind when someone invites you to *dinner*? Do you picture having a nice hearty meal? Or, do you picture yourself getting a hamburger from a fast food restaurant?

Webster's New Collegiate Dictionary defines *dinner* as, *"the principal meal of the day, eaten about midday or in the evening."*

I know people who refer to their midday meal as *dinner*, no matter how large or small that meal is. Other people I know use the term *dinner* to describe their evening meal. So which meal is *dinner*?

If someone invites you to *dinner*, one thing you can know for sure is you will be eating a meal, but do you picture that meal being at midday or in the evening? Will it be a large meal or a sandwich? You may have one picture in mind, but your host may have a different one. Their use of the word *dinner* may follow Webster's definition or it may not. You may expect a full course meal but be served a bowl of soup. It helps to know what your host means by the word *dinner* so your expectations are the same as theirs.

The same is true when Christians discuss the Holy Spirit. For example, what do you think of when you hear the word, *tongues*? That term brings a different picture to different people's minds. That is because different groups of Christians have their own definition for that word and for other terms relating to the person and work of the Holy Spirit. The problem is those definitions vary widely. That causes a lot of confusion and misunderstanding.

It is very important to understand just because someone uses the same terms as you, that person may not mean the same thing you do. There will be times when you will be talking with someone else and think you are talking about the same thing, but then, when you learn their definition of those words, you realize they mean something entirely different from what you thought they meant. Always find out what someone means by the terms he or she uses, especially when discussing the Holy Spirit.

Every field of study has its own technical jargon. When I attended Community College, I studied sociology, anthropology and psychology. Those subjects had impressive technical names. When I went to Bible College, I studied theology and discovered it has its own impressive words, like soteriology, eschatology, ecclesiology and pneumatology. Those are all technical terms for some major areas of doctrine.

This book takes an in-depth look at the field of pneumatology. The term, **pneumatology**, is derived from the Greek word, **pneuma**, which means, *spirit, wind or breath.* It is the technical name for the doctrine of the Holy Spirit.

A proper study of pneumatology will look at **both** the **Person** and **Work** of the Holy Spirit. To understand the Holy Spirit, you need to understand **Who He Is** and **What He Does**.

There is a lot of crossover between pneumatology and other areas of doctrine, such as soteriology (*the doctrine of salvation*) and ecclesiology (*the doctrine of the church*).

The Warning: Do Not Be Ignorant

The study of the Holy Spirit has been a controversial subject down through the ages. That controversy became more intense in the later part of the twentieth century, with the birth of the **Charismatic Movement**.

Though I was part of the Charismatic Movement when it first started, I did not become aware of the intense conflict and drastic division among believers over the doctrine of the Holy Spirit, until I was a young Bible College student. Ever since then, I have sadly seen believers all around the world bitterly divided over this doctrine. The conflict is so intense it often leads to intolerance and almost hatred, among some, toward those who hold different positions.

Satan is happy when believers have conflicts. He wants Christians divided or ignorant. That is especially true regarding the teaching of the Holy Spirit. Satan knows when believers understand *who* the Holy Spirit is, and know *what* God wants to do in their lives, they will unite, serve the Lord, and become a powerful force Satan cannot defeat.

God knew there would be this controversy. He knew people would have problems understanding this important doctrine. So right at the beginning of the teaching on things relating to the Holy Spirit, He clearly warns us not to be *ignorant*.

> Now concerning spiritual *gifts [pneumatikon]*, brethren,
> I would not have you ignorant *[agnoein]*.
> *1 Corinthians 12:1*

Greek was the language used to write most of the New Testament. The word *ignorant*, in this passage, is the translation of the Greek word, **agnoein**. It means *to be unsure*. We get our word, *agnostic* from this. An agnostic is one who says they are not sure whether God exists or not. In this verse, God says, He does not want us to be *unsure* (**agnoein**) about the teaching relating to the Holy Spirit. He wants us to *understand with certainty* this very important doctrine. What you believe about the Holy Spirit greatly affects your life and those around you.

It is important to understand the specific word, *gifts*, in 1 Corinthians 12:1, does not appear in the Greek manuscripts. Notice the word *gifts,* appears in the passage in italics in most translations. When a word appears in italics in the Bible that means it was not in the original manuscripts. The translators added the *italicized words*; to try to give the reader, what they felt was a better sense of what the passage meant.

The English words, *spiritual gifts*, in 1 Corinthians 12:1, translate the Greek word, **pneumatikon. Pneumatikon** is the Greek word, which means, *things relating to the Holy Spirit*. If this passage were referring only to *spiritual gifts*, it would use the Greek word **charismaton**, which specifically means, *spiritual gifts*. Though *spiritual gifts* are part of the context in 1

Corinthians 12, and should rightly be included in this warning, the word for *spiritual gifts* (**charismaton**) was not used in the original text because the scope of this warning includes more than just *spiritual gifts*. The warning extends to the whole realm of *pneumatikon,* things relating to the Holy Spirit.

The fact we cannot see the Holy Spirit makes it a little more difficult to understand Him. As humans, we find it easier to believe what we can see and touch. Pneumatology is a study of an aspect of Christianity, beyond the realm of human senses; it concerns something, which is supernatural.

If Christians realized it is only natural for a supernatural God to work in supernatural ways, it could transform their lives and help them understand this and other doctrines in the Bible. We have a tendency to de-supernaturalize God. We unconsciously tend to strip Him of His supernatural essence, especially in His personal dealings with us. Hence, too often we miss His supernatural power in our lives.

Understanding the Biblical teaching on the Holy Spirit is essential to live a victorious Christian life. Without the Holy Spirit, it is impossible to live the Christian life at all. Without the Holy Spirit, we could not be saved, nor could we ever be victorious in the spiritual warfare we face each day. Without the Holy Spirit, we also would never know the comfort, leading and assurance God desires to give us continually.

It is interesting to note though God gives us a specific warning, not to be ignorant about things pertaining to the Holy Spirit, various schools of thought, completely at odds with each other, have developed over the years, regarding pneumatology. Obviously, many people misunderstand this important doctrine.

The controversy over the Holy Spirit covers a broad range of beliefs. Some, who claim to be Christians, deny the Holy Spirit is God. Some believe the Holy Spirit is God, but disagree about *How* He works. Many disagree with *How* and *When* the Holy Spirit *Indwells* the believer, and over *How* He works in the lives of Believers. All these divergent viewpoints can, and must, be resolved.

The following is a brief look at some of the more prominent divergent viewpoints regarding the Person and Work of the Holy

Spirit. The book deals with many of these in more detail in other chapters.

Unitarianism or Non-Trinitarianism

Some religious groups use the term, *Christian* to identify themselves, yet do not believe the Holy Spirit is God. They totally dismiss the personhood of the Holy Spirit. These are *Non-Trinitarians*.

Unitarians are a Non-Trinitarian group. They believe in God, but they do not believe God is a Trinity. They do not believe Jesus was God. They teach Jesus was a divine (*godly but not God)* man, and say all men can be divine (*godly*).

They also do not believe the Holy Spirit is God, nor do they believe in the personality of the Holy Spirit. They believe such terms as, *the Holy Spirit,* does not speak of the Holy Spirit as a distinct person in the Trinity, but rather speaks of a Non-Trinitarian God, who is a spirit, presence or force.

Some Unitarians claim their roots come from the early Christian *Gnostics.* Gnostics taught they had a special knowledge of life and God. They opposed the Judeo and early Christian teachings about the nature of God. To them, God was more of a mystical force than a person. Early Church leaders addressed the teachings of Gnostics as heresy.

Historically, the teaching held by today's Unitarian groups did not surface until the Protestant Reformation. They opposed some of the teachings of the Reformers and became known as *Anti-Trinitarians* and *Socinians.*

Since the Reformation, a few different groups followed the Unitarian teaching. A formal church group did not adopt the name *Unitarian*, until 1819, in Boston, Massachusetts.

The *Unitarian Church* believes in the goodness of man and believes all of humankind will be saved. They do not believe in the inerrancy of the Bible. *Inerrancy is the teaching that the Bible is without error.* Unitarians believe the Bible is inspired, only in the sense that it is inspiring as are the works of authors such as William Shakespeare. The author, Ralph Waldo Emerson, was a noted Unitarian.

Though there is an organized body known as *Unitarians*, other groups, and many cults, hold to the Non-Trinitarian, Unitarian concept of God, thus dismissing the deity of Christ and the personhood of the Holy Spirit.

Some Non-Trinitarian Groups Include:

O   **Christadelphians** *(Brethren of Christ)*
Not to be confused with the Brethren.

O   **Church of Christ Scientist** *(Christian Science)*

O   **Jehovah's Witnesses**

O   **Mormons** *(Church of Jesus Christ of the Latter Day Saints)*

O   **The Unification Church**
Followers of Rev. Sun Myung Moon

O   **Some of the Christian Churches** *(Disciples of Christ)*.

O   **Some of the Church of God groups, and others**.

The Worldwide Church of God *(Armstrongism)* founded by Herbert W. Armstrong, in the late 1930's was originally a Non-Trinitarian group. That church made a major doctrinal change in the mid 1990's, and embraced the Biblical teaching of the Trinity.

Calvinism & Arminianism

All evangelical groups believe in the Triune God (*Three in One*). They recognize the deity of Christ, the personhood of the Holy Spirit and recognize the Holy Spirit as God. They agree on *Who* the Holy Spirit is, but differ on *How* He *Works*. It is mainly, *How the Holy Spirit Works*, which has become the point of controversy among evangelicals.

In Evangelical circles, there are two major controversies regarding the Holy Spirit. There is the teaching of the *Calvinist* versus the *Arminianist* and the teaching of the *Pentecostals* and

Charismatics versus the *Non-Pentecostals* and *Non-Charismatics.*

Briefly put, *Calvinism* and *Arminianism* differ on the work of the Holy Spirit in relationship to *salvation* and the *permanency* of that salvation. *Calvinism* teaches the Holy Spirit works in a general way among all humankind and in a special way for a limited group, whom they believe God predetermined to be heirs of salvation. *Arminianism*, on the other hand, teaches the Holy Spirit works in a general way among all people then conditionally *indwells* those who trust Christ. The chapter in this book on *The Holy Spirit and Salvation* addresses those issues.

Pentecostals & Charismatics

The other major area of controversy in Evangelical circles, regarding the Holy Spirit, is that of the *Pentecostals* and *Charismatics* versus the *Non-Pentecostals* and *Non-Charismatics.*

It is important to note, though the teachings of *Pentecostals* and *Charismatics* are similar, they are two distinct groups. They both believe in a second fuller work of the Holy Spirit, in the life of a believer, which occurs subsequent to (*after*) salvation.

Pentecostals believe a person does not fully receive the Holy Spirit until some point after one is a recipient of salvation. They often hold to an *Arminian* interpretation of the work of the Holy Spirit in relation to salvation. Many *Pentecostals*, but not all, believe it is possible for a person to lose their salvation.

Pentecostals use the term, *receiving the Holy Spirit.* Specifically what *receiving the Holy Spirit* means, can vary greatly from one *Pentecostal* group to another.

Most *Pentecostals* believe the evidence of *receiving the Holy Spirit* is speaking in ecstatic *(mystical)* utterances (which they usually refer to as *tongues*).

Charismatics are similar to the *Pentecostals* in some ways, but are a distinct group with various branches. The *Charismatic Movement* sprung directly out of mainline *non-Pentecostal* groups. It includes *Calvinists* and *Arminianists.* At first,

Charismatics were called *Neo-Pentecostals (New Pentecostals).* After a while, people gave them the name *Charismatics.* Most *Charismatics* believe in a work of the Holy Spirit subsequent to (*after*) salvation, which each believer should seek if they wish to find true fulfillment in Christ.

The *key difference* between the *Pentecostals* and *Charismatics* is *Pentecostals* believe speaking in tongues *is the evidence* of that subsequent work of the Holy Spirit. *Charismatics* on the other hand believe the evidence of that subsequent work of the Holy Spirit can occur that way or in a variety of other ways. *Charismatics* believe speaking in ecstatic utterances *(which they call tongues),* is only one of a variety of evidences of this second work of the Holy Spirit. Unlike the *Pentecostals,* they do not all believe everyone who has this second work of the Holy Spirit must speak in *tongues.*

Many *Charismatics* mistakenly identify themselves as *Pentecostals* because of a lack of understanding of the distinction between the *Pentecostals* and *Charismatics.*

Conservative Christianity's Reaction

Reaction to the controversy surrounding the Holy Spirit varies between Conservative Evangelical and Fundamental Christians. The following are some of reactions I observed:

○ **Seek Not, Forbid Not** – When some look at the *Pentecostal* and *Charismatic* Movements, they see the souls saved and lives changed and decide these movements must be of God. Though they do not personally accept those positions, they choose not to challenge them. These people encourage others to make up their own minds. They often take what is known as a, *seek not, forbid not,* attitude towards the *Pentecostal* or *Charismatic* experience.

○ **Avoid the Issue** - Some look at the controversy between *Calvinist* and *Arminianist,* and between *Pentecostal* and *Non Pentecostal,* and know where they stand, but cannot set forth their position in a clear concise way. They feel awkward discussing these issues and prefer to avoid them. Often they do not mention the *Holy Spirit, Calvinism, Tongues, Healing*, or any other words which may bring these subjects to the forefront.

O **Explain Them Away** - Some look at the contemporary movements, which give prominence to the Holy Spirit, and attempt to explain away the beliefs and practices of these movements. This is a flawed reaction because it accepts contemporary presuppositions or definitions regarding the Holy Spirit and His Work, then looks at the Bible, and tries to explain them away. People who take this stance need to look carefully at the clear context of the Word of God, accept the *Biblical* definitions, then evaluate the modern issues, in light of the Word of God, rather than evaluate the Word of God in light of these modern issues.

O **Strongly Oppose** - Others take a strong stand on these issues and verbally chastise others who differ with them. Some even go as far as to question the salvation of others with differing viewpoints.

I believe all of these reactions may be sincere, but are sincerely wrong. We need to take a careful look at the Biblical teaching regarding the Holy Spirit and arrive at the common ground God wants us to have.

Conclusion

There is a lot of controversy in Christian circles involving the doctrine of the Holy Spirit. God does not want us to have so much division. If God says we should not be ignorant about the doctrine of the Holy Spirit, then we should be able to arrive at a proper understanding of this important doctrine and find agreement. We cannot agree to disagree.

Dr. Larry A. Maxwell

We can, and must, understand this important doctrine. We must not *react* to the controversy over the Holy Spirit. We must *respond* to these issues regarding the Person and Work of the Holy Spirit. We must find the Biblical answers. We can and must face these issues head on, with an open heart and mind.

It is my prayer, as you look at the various aspects of this important doctrine, this study will help resolve some of the controversy.

In the next chapter, we will take a careful look at *Who the Holy Spirit Is*. Later in this book, we will look at *What He Does*.

CHAPTER ONE
QUESTIONS

Verse to Memorize: 1 Corinthians 12:1

1.1 What is Pneumatology?

1.2 What warning does God give us regarding things, which pertain to the Holy Spirit?

1.3 What is the *Unitarian* or *Non-Trinitarian* viewpoint of the Holy Spirit?

1.4 Do *Calvinists* and *Arminianists* differ on *Who the Holy Spirit Is* or on *How the Holy Spirit Works*?

1.5 What is one of the distinguishing marks of the *Pentecostal* viewpoint regarding the Holy Spirit and the believer?

1.6 What are some of the wrong ways people react to the controversy surrounding the Holy Spirit?

QUESTIONS FOR ADDITIONAL THOUGHT

1.7 What are some *Non-Trinitarian* groups and how do they view the Holy Spirit?

1.8 How does a *Charismatic* differ from a *Pentecostal*?

1.9 How should we respond to the controversy surrounding the Holy Spirit?

Dr. Larry A. Maxwell

CHAPTER TWO

Who is The Holy Spirit?

The Holy Spirit & The Trinity

The word Trinity means, *three in one.* One reason Non-Trinitarian groups dispute the teaching of the Trinity is because the English word, *Trinity* does not appear in the Bible. The English word *incarnation* does not appear in the Bible either, yet most people do not dispute that as a valid doctrine. Neither does the English word *divinity* appear in the Bible. Nor does the word *synagogue* appear anywhere in the Old Testament, yet we know they existed.

Trinity is a technical theological word used to describe the nature of God. Though the English word *Trinity* does not appear in the Bible, you will find the concept and teaching of a Triune God throughout the Word of God, in both the Old and New Testaments.

The concept of the Trinity is clearly not a doctrine conceived by man. It would not make any sense for someone to concoct such a difficult doctrine to understand.

It is important to remember God is infinite and we are finite. Our understanding is limited when it comes to spiritual things. Our natural language has a hard time fully expressing spiritual concepts much less the nature and character and concept or an infinite God (1 Corinthians 2:6-16).

Even though we may not fully understand the Trinity, we can understand certain aspects about it.

In referring to the Trinity as a whole, some use the word *Godhead.* The Godhead is not three individuals, if it was, that would be a *triad* or *tri-theism.* Nor is the Godhead one God, who reveals himself at different times in different roles, that is called *modalism.*

The God of the Bible is one God, comprised of three distinct persons, God the Father, God the Son and God the Holy Spirit. The three are eternal and co-equal in substance *(that which they are comprised of, their essence)*, but are distinct in subsistence *(in their existence or being).* The Holy Spirit is the third person of the Trinity. He is as much God as God the Father and God the Son. He is a *distinct person*, though not a *distinct God.*

Earthly illustrations fall short of explaining the Trinity. Some compare the Trinity to the sun, which is at the center of our solar system. We feel the sun's warmth *(similar to God the Holy Spirit)*, we see its light *(light is a word used to describe God the Son)*, yet we know there is more substance to it which we cannot see with the naked eye *(similar to God the Father)*. Each of those aspects of the sun has its own characteristics, which are physically different and, which you can measure and identify as unique.

One of the strongest proofs for the existence of the Trinity comes from the combination of plural and singular words used for God in the Bible.

In Genesis 1:1, the very first verse in the Bible, the Hebrew word, *Elohim*, is used for God.

> In the beginning God *[Elohim]* created the heaven and
> the earth.   Genesis 1:1

The word *Elohim* has the ending, *im*, which is a plural ending in Hebrew. In Genesis 1:1, the singular verb, *created,* follows the plural word *Elohim*. That means one God, with a plural nature, did the creating.

Another important passage, which reinforces the concept of the Trinity, is Deuteronomy 6:4. That passage of *Torah* is the *Shema*. Devout Jews recite the *Shema* daily, as a prayer.

In the Jewish community where I grew up, many of my friends recited that prayer. It is one of the foundation stones of faith for Judaism. It declares the God of Israel is totally unique and is only one God, as opposed to the multiplicity of gods worshipped by the nations around them. It is interesting to note the combination of plural and singular words, used for God, in Deuteronomy 6:4.

Echad Yahweh Elohenu Yahweh Israel Shema
[Read this Hebrew passage from right to left.]

This passage says *Hear Israel, God, our God, God He is One.* The Hebrew word **YHWH**, is written as *Yahweh*. Due to the supreme reverence for the name of God, scholars may substitute the word *Adonai* in its place, or sometimes G-D, to make sure they would not mistake pronouncing God's name. The word **YHWH**, is also translated by some as *Jehovah (though most scholars agree it is not possible to get that transliteration from the Hebrew).*

The King James Bible translates **YHWH** as **LORD** (*all capital letters*). This is the formal singular name for God.

Elohenu, one of the other words in this passage, is the possessive plural of *Elohim*, the plural name for God. *Echad*, means one, but in the same sense a husband and wife *(two different persons)* are one (Genesis 2:24).

God clearly uses a combination of singular and plural words to describe Himself. The carefully chosen words in the *Shema* clearly teach us there is one God who has a plural nature, yet who is still only one God. This is a very strong passage to reinforce the teaching of the Triune God, the Three in One.

The identity of the members of the Godhead is found in passages such as Matthew 28:18-20, 2 Corinthians 13:14, 1 Corinthians 12:4-6 and 1 John 5:7. Those passages further reinforce the Triune nature of God.

> Go ye therefore, and teach all nations, baptizing them in the name of the **Father**, and of the **Son**, and of the **Holy Ghost**.   Matthew 28:19

> The grace of the **Lord Jesus Christ**, and the love of **God**, and the communion of the **Holy Ghost**, be with you all. Amen.   2 Corinthians 13:14

> Now there are diversities of gifts, but the same **Spirit**. And there are differences of administrations, but the same **Lord**. And there are diversities of operations, but it is the same **God** which worketh all in all.
>   1 Corinthians 12:4-6

> For there are three that bear record in heaven, the **Father**, the **Word** [*Jesus*], and the **Holy Ghost**: and these three are one.   1 John 5:7

It is obvious from the Scriptures the Holy Spirit is God. As God, He shares all the attributes of God.

Attributes of the Holy Spirit

The Scriptures have much to say about the Holy Spirit. The following is a brief look at some of His attributes:

1.   He Has Life (Romans 8:2).

> For the law of the Spirit of life in Christ Jesus hath made me free from the law of sin and death.
>
> Romans 8:2

The Holy Spirit has life. He is not some inanimate object or force. He has life, in and of Himself. It is exciting to know He wants to share that life with us.

2.   He is a Person (John 14:16-17; 15:26).

> And I will pray the Father, and He shall give you another Comforter, that He may abide with you forever, even the Spirit of Truth...   John 14:16-17a

> But when the Comforter is come, whom I will send unto you from the Father, even the Spirit of Truth, which proceedeth from the Father, He shall testify of me.
>
> John 15:26-27

The word *Comforter* is the translation of the Greek word, *parakletos*. This word always refers to a person, not an inanimate power or force.

The word *another,* is the translation of the Greek word, *allon*, which indicates *one like myself.* This clearly indicates the Holy Spirit is a person. He is *Another Comforter, like* the Father and the Son. I find it amazing such a God wants to have a personal relationship with you and me.

3.   He Possesses Intelligence (1 Corinthians 12:8; Isaiah 11:2-3; Nehemiah 9:20; 1 Peter 1:11; 2 Peter 1:21).

> And the Spirit of the LORD shall rest upon Him, the
> Spirit of wisdom and understanding, the Spirit of counsel
> and might, the Spirit of knowledge and the fear of the
> LORD.   Isaiah 11:2

> For the prophesy came not in old time by the will of man:
> but holy men of God spake as they were moved by the
> Holy Ghost.   2 Peter 1:21

The Holy Spirit is not some unintelligent, unthinking force or being. He has the ability to understand and reason. Because He is intelligent, He can, and has, and will personally communicate with us, in a way we can understand.

4.   He Possesses a Sovereign Will (1 Corinthians 12:11).

> But all these worketh that one and the selfsame Spirit,
> dividing to every man severally as He will.
>   1 Corinthians 12:11

The Holy Spirit does as He wills. He is not a subservient messenger. As God, He can exercise His sovereign will on humankind. His will is always good. He wants us to know His will and experience the joy of doing it.

It is He who sovereignly gives results when we minister for God in the power of the Holy Spirit.

5.   He Possesses Power (Romans 15:13,19; Zechariah 4:6; Isaiah 11:2; Ephesians 3:16).

> Now the God of hope fill you with all joy and peace in
> believing, that ye may abound in hope, through the power
> of the Holy Ghost.   Romans 15:13

> Then he answered and spake unto me saying, This is the
> word of the LORD unto Zerubbabel, saying, Not by
> might, nor by power, but by my Spirit, saith the LORD
> of Hosts.   Zechariah 4:6

The Holy Spirit is not weak. He is God and has almighty, omnipotent power. His power is far greater than any other power on earth.

It is exciting to know the Holy Spirit can, and wants to, convey a measure of His power to man. That power gives us hope, which can fill us with joy and peace. We need to believe Him and allow His power to work in our lives.

6. He Possesses Knowledge (1 Corinthians 2:10-12).

But God hath revealed them unto us by His Spirit: for the Spirit searcheth all things, yea, the deep things of God. For what man knoweth the things of a man, save the spirit of man which is in him? Even so the things of God knoweth no man, but the Spirit of God.

1 Corinthians 2:10-11

The Holy Spirit not only has intelligence *(the ability to reason)*, He also has all knowledge about God and man. No one has the amount of information the Holy Spirit does, nor can anyone understand as the Holy Spirit does. He has the answer to any question you will ever have and can give you the information you need.

7. He is Omniscient (1 Corinthians 2:10).

But God hath revealed them unto us by His Spirit: for the Spirit searcheth all things, yea, the deep things of God.

1 Corinthians 2:10

Omniscient means, *He is all knowing and knows everything.* Nothing takes Him by surprise. The Holy Spirit knows everything. It is comforting to know He knows what we are going through.

8. He is Omnipresent (Psalm 139:7-10).

Whither shall I go from the Spirit? Or whither shall I flee from Thy presence? If I ascend up into heaven, Thou art there: if I make my bed in hell, behold, Thou art there.

Psalm 139:7-8

Omnipresent means, *being in all places at the same time.* Only God possesses this characteristic. Other spiritual beings like angels, demons and Satan, can only be in one place at a time. Because the Holy Spirit is God and can be everywhere at all times, it means He is always there to help you. This means, He can *save* all who call on the Lord, at any time, in any place.

9.   He is Eternal (Hebrews 9:14).

How much more shall the blood of Christ, who through the eternal Spirit offered Himself without spot to God, purge your conscience from dead works to serve the living God?   Hebrews 9:14

The Holy Spirit is eternal. He does not have a beginning or an end. He has always been there and always will be. I do not have to worry about my Helper ceasing to exist.

10.   He is Holy (Ephesians 4:30).

And grieve not the Holy Spirit of God, whereby ye are sealed unto the day of redemption.

Ephesians 4:30

Above all, the Holy Spirit is Holy *(hagios)*. He is spiritually whole. There is not any imperfection or sin in Him. If we allow Him to work in our lives, He can produce His holiness in us. He can help us with our imperfections and free us from sin, which continually seeks to enslave us.

11.   He Possesses Love (Romans 15:30).

Now I beseech you, brethren, for the Lord Jesus Christ's sake, and for the love of the Spirit, that ye strive together with me in your prayers to God for me.

Romans 15:30

The Holy Spirit loves us. He is not a cruel, uncaring force. He is a personal loving God who cares for you and wants to help you.

12.   He Speaks (Acts 13:2).

As they ministered to the Lord, and fasted, the Holy Ghost said, Separate me Barnabas and Saul for the work whereunto I have called them.   Acts 13:2

The Holy Spirit communicates with man. He has spoken. He usually communicates with man by making the Word of

God *(the Bible)* come alive in our hearts as we read it, or as we hear it taught, preached or sung.

13.   He May Be Grieved (Ephesians 4:30).

> And grieve not the Holy Spirit of God, whereby ye are sealed unto the day of redemption.   Ephesians 4:30

Only someone who loves another can be grieved *(saddened or harmed)*. The reason our words and actions can grieve the Holy Spirit is because He loves us. He intensely cares for us. That should motivate us to avoid grieving Him.

14.   He May Be Tested (Acts 5:9).

> Then said Peter unto her, How is it that ye have agreed to tempt *[test]* the Spirit of the Lord.   Acts 5:9a

The Holy Spirit responds to our thoughts or actions. When we follow, or disobey Scripture, we put Him to the test and He responds. The Holy Spirit does not let our thoughts or actions go unheeded. He blesses obedience and punishes disobedience.

15.   He May Be Resisted (Acts 7:51).

> Ye stiffnecked and uncircumcised in heart and ears, ye do always resist the Holy Ghost: as your fathers did, so do ye.   Acts 7:51

Though the Holy Spirit is all-powerful *(omnipotent)*, He gives us a choice to obey His leading or not. It is possible to stop listening to Him and not obey His will. Too often, we resist His will and put our own will first.

16.   He May Be Blasphemed (Mark 3:28-30).

> But he that shall blaspheme against the Holy Ghost hath never forgiveness, but is in danger of mortal damnation.
> Mark 3:29

To blaspheme means to assail someone verbally. It is possible to assail the Holy Spirit verbally. This is a very serious sin, which can prevent one from initiating a personal relationship with God.

Names Used in the Bible for the Holy Spirit

There are two primary names used for the Holy Spirit in the Bible. In the Old Testament, the Hebrew word, **ruach**, is used. It means, *Spirit* (Ghost). In the New Testament, the Greek word, **pneuma**, is used. It also means, *Spirit* (Ghost).

The words, *Spirit* and *Ghost*, are actually synonyms. In this study, we use the designation *Holy Spirit* instead of the *Holy Ghost*. This is because the meaning of the word *ghost* has become associated with the incorrect picture of the spirits of dead people returning to this earth to haunt or guide the living.

There is a variety of other names used in the Bible for the Holy Spirit. Each of these names is significant. As we look at each one, it can help give us a better understanding about the person of the Holy Spirit.

1.   The Holy Ghost (Luke 4:1-2).

> And Jesus being full of the Holy *[hagios]* Ghost *[pneuma]* returned from the Jordan, and was led by the Spirit into the wilderness.   Luke 4:1

Here He is not just called the Ghost (*Spirit*); He is called the Holy *(hagios)* Ghost. This is because He is a holy spiritual being and only He makes others holy.

2.   The Holy Spirit of God (Ephesians 4:30).

> And grieve not the Holy Spirit of God, whereby ye are sealed unto the day of redemption.
> Ephesians 4:30

The Holy Spirit is not just a spirit, which is holy; He is the very spirit of the Holy God. God's holiness dwells with us through the Holy Spirit.

3.   The Spirit of God (Exodus 31:3).

> And I have filled him with the Spirit of God, in wisdom, and in understanding, and in knowledge, and in all manner of workmanship.   Exodus 31:3

As the Spirit of God, the Holy Spirit allows us to

experience the joy of God residing in our hearts.

4.   God (Acts 5:3-4; 1 Corinthians 3:16).

> Know ye not that ye are the temple of God, and that the Spirit of God dwelleth in you?   1 Corinthians 3:16

The Holy Spirit is clearly God. When He lives in us, God is living in our hearts. God does not dwell in physical buildings in any special way. Believers are His temple. Our bodies are the place He desires to *indwell*.

5.   Spirit of the Lord (2 Corinthians 3:17).

> Now the Lord is that Spirit: and where the Spirit of the Lord is, there is Liberty.   2 Corinthians 3:17

As the Spirit of the Lord, the Holy Spirit allows us to become members of God's kingdom. When we become part of His Kingdom, God becomes our Lord and King. We no longer have to be slaves to sin, our old master. We are free from the bondage of sin to become servants to a new Lord.

6.   The Spirit of Christ (1 Peter 1:10-11)

> Searching what, or what manner of time the Spirit of Christ which was in them did signify, when it testified beforehand the sufferings of Christ, and the glory that should follow.   1 Peter 1:11

Before Christ came to earth as the God-Man, it was through the Holy Spirit moving *upon* man that Christ was able to convey His will to man.

7.   The Spirit of Jehovah (YHWH) (Judges 6:34).

> But the Spirit of the LORD [YHWH] came upon Gideon, and he blew a trumpet; and Abiezer was gathered after him.   Judges 6:34

As the Spirit of Jehovah *(more properly translated as Yahweh)*, the Holy Spirit shows us He is the Spirit not just for the Gentiles, but for Israel too. YHWH *(Yahweh)* is the most revered name for God among the Jewish people.

8.   The Holy Spirit of Promise (Ephesians 1:13).

> In whom ye also trusted, after that ye heard the word of truth, the gospel of your salvation: in whom after that ye believed, ye were sealed with that Holy Spirit of promise.
> Ephesians 1:13

He is the Holy Spirit of Promise. In the Old Testament, God promised His people a rest. Some interpreted this to mean the Promised Land. In one sense, they did get rest in that land. However, there is a greater rest for God's people. When we receive the Holy Spirit and allow Him to control our lives, we can have rest from the struggle of trying to live for God in the flesh. This is an exciting new dimension to life, which became available to believers, when the promised Holy Spirit came to *indwell* man.

9.   The Seven Spirits (Revelation 1:4; 4:5; Isaiah 11:2).

> John to the seven churches which are in Asia: Grace be unto you, and peace, from Him which is, and which was and which is to come; and from the seven spirits which are before His throne.
> Revelation 1:4

The Seven Spirits is a reference to Isaiah 11:2, where the Holy Spirit is identified as manifesting Himself in a seven-fold way. There we see Him as the spirit of the *LORD*, of *wisdom*, of *understanding*, of *counsel*, of *might*, of *knowledge* and of *the fear of the Lord*. These are seven important characteristics He wants us to know about Him.

10.   The Spirit of Glory and of God (1 Peter 4:14).

> If ye be reproached for the name of Christ, happy are ye; for the Spirit of Glory and of God resteth upon you: on their part He is evil spoken of, but on your part He is glorified.
> 1 Peter 4:14

As the Spirit of Glory and of God, we learn it was the Holy Spirit, who filled the tabernacle with God's glorious presence in the Old Testament. In this same way, He came to the shepherds on the hillside, outside of Bethlehem, and shone the glory of God around them.

It is His desire to fill the church with that same glory (Ephesians 3:20-21).

11. The Spirit of Holiness (Romans 1:4).

And declared to be the Son of God with power, according to the Spirit of Holiness, by the resurrection from the dead.   Romans 1:4

He is the Spirit of Holiness. Without Him, we can never approach the presence of the Holy God but with Him, we have full access to God.

12. The Holy One (1 John 2:20).

But ye have an unction *[anointing]* from the Holy One, and ye know all things.   1 John 2:20

The Holy Spirit is The Holy *(hagios)* One. Everything we ever need to know about what it means to be holy *(hagios)* can be found in Him.

He anoints us in such a way that all we have to do is ask Him to teach us and help make us holy and He will.

13. The Spirit of Wisdom (Exodus 28:3; Ephesians 1:17).

And thou shalt speak unto all that are wise-hearted, whom I have filled with the Spirit of Wisdom...
                                                    Exodus 28:3a

As the Spirit of Wisdom, the Holy Spirit is able to convey to us the practical information *(wisdom)* we need to live our lives according to His will. We do not have to wander around without understanding.

14. The Spirit of Truth (John 14:17).

Even the Spirit of Truth; whom the world cannot receive, because it seeth Him not, neither knoweth Him: but ye know Him; for He dwelleth with you, and shall be in you.
                                                    John 14:17

This word *truth* is in the qualitative genitive form in this verse. That is a grammatical way of indicating He is the truth *in person.* Everyone wants to know truth. We can find everything we need to know about truth in Him and we can know that personally.

15.   The Free Spirit (Psalm 51:12).

> Restore unto me the joy of thy salvation; and uphold me
> with thy Free Spirit.   Psalm 51:12

This can indicate there is nothing we can do to earn the Holy Spirit; He is freely given to us. This also means He is free and not bound.

This also reminds us we can find true freedom in a personal relationship with God, through the Holy Spirit.

16.   The Spirit of Grace (Hebrews 10:29).

> Of how much sorer punishment, suppose ye, shall he be
> thought worthy, who hath trodden under foot the Son of
> God, and hath counted the blood of the covenant,
> wherewith he was sanctified, an unholy thing, and hath
> done despite unto the Spirit of Grace.
>   Hebrews 10:29

As the Spirit of Grace, the Holy Spirit can give us blessings we do not deserve *(grace).*

Our salvation, and all the benefits God gives us, is undeserved. By the grace of God, He gives them to us through the Holy Spirit.

17.   The Spirit of Life (Romans 8:2).

> For the law of the Spirit of Life in Christ Jesus hath made
> me free from the law of sin and death.
>   Romans 8:2

As the Spirit of Life, the Holy Spirit can give us life eternal. That is life, which keeps on living.

You do not have to wait until you die to have eternal life. That life becomes yours, through the Holy Spirit, the moment you are saved.

18. **The Comforter/Helper** (John 14:16, 26; 15:26; 16:7).

And I will pray the Father, and He shall give you another Comforter, that he may abide with you forever.
John 14:16

The word translated, *Comforter,* is the Greek word, **parakletos**. It means *a person called to alongside in order to help*. He is the best comforter we could ever have. The Holy Spirit cares about us and wants to comfort and help us. He is always there, by our side, when we need Him.

Symbols of the Holy Spirit

Besides being referred to by specific names, the Holy Spirit is also identified symbolically in the Scriptures as:

1. **A Dove** (Luke 3:21-22; Mark 1:10-11; John 1:32-34).

And the Holy Ghost descended in a bodily shape like a dove upon Him, and a voice came from heaven, which said, Thou art my beloved Son; in Thee I am well pleased.
Luke 3:22

People often make a mistake when they portray the baptism of Jesus by John the Baptist. The show a dove come down and land *upon* Jesus. The Holy Spirit did not *become* a dove but He appeared in a physical form, which looked *like (resembling)* a dove. The dove has since been a symbol of peace through the presence of God.

2. **Water** (Isaiah 44:3; John 7:38-39).

I will pour water upon him that is thirsty, and floods upon the dry ground: I will pour my Spirit upon thy seed, and my blessing upon thy offspring.
Isaiah 44:3

Physically, water is both *essential* and *refreshing* to life. In the same way, spiritually, the Holy Spirit is *essential* for us to have eternal life. He also can *refresh* us daily, both physically and spiritually.

40

3.   Oil (1 Samuel 16:13; Isaiah 61:1; James 5:14)

> Then Samuel took the horn of oil, and anointed him in
> the midst of his brethren: and the Spirit of the LORD
> came upon David from that day forward. So Samuel rose
> up and went to Ramah.   1 Samuel 16:13

> Is any sick among you? let him call for the elders of the
> church; and let them pray over him, anointing him with
> oil in the name of the Lord.   James 5:14

In the Old Testament, they used oil to anoint the kings
and priests. That oil was a symbol of the Holy Spirit.

Some believe the anointing with oil in the passage in
James refers to symbolically committing the person to the
Holy Spirit. Some believe the anointing with oil in that
passage means using medicine *(like the medicinal oils used
in Bible times)*, coupled with prayer.

4.   Wind (Ezekiel 37:9,14; Acts 2:2; John 3:3-8).

> The wind bloweth where it listeth, and thou hearest the
> sound thereof, but canst not tell whence it cometh, and
> whither it goeth: so is every one that is born of the Spirit.
>   John 3:8

> And suddenly there came a sound from heaven as of a
> rushing mighty wind, and it filled all the house where
> they were sitting...and they were all filled with the Holy
> Ghost...   Acts 2:2, 4

The Holy Spirit is compared to the wind, which is not
seen, but which is clearly felt. Though the Holy Spirit is not
seen, He clearly brings a fresh breath of life.

Notice in Acts 2:2-4 a *sound* came from heaven *as of* a
rushing mighty wind. It was a sound *like* a wind.

5.   Fire (Acts 2:3-4).

> And there appeared unto them cloven tongues like as of
> fire, and it sat upon each of them. And they were filled
> with the Holy Ghost, and began to speak with other
> tongues, as the Spirit gave them utterance.
>   Acts 2:3-4

In the Bible, they often used fire for sacrifices and for purification. In the same way, the Holy Spirit purifies us and helps us be a living acceptable sacrifice for the Lord (Romans 12:1-2).

6.   Clothing (Luke 24:49; Ephesians 4:24; 6:11).

And behold, I send the promise of my Father upon you: but tarry ye in the city of Jerusalem, until ye be endowed [*clothed*] with power from on high.

Luke 24:49

As one puts on clothing, to make oneself presentable before others, we must determine to put on the Holy Spirit, to allow Him to *empower* us so we can be spiritually presentable.

Works of the Holy Spirit

The Holy Spirit is very active, throughout the Scripture and today. The following are brief descriptions of some of the works in the Bible which He had an active part:

1.   Creation (Genesis 1:1-2; Psalm 104:30; Job 33:4).

Thou sendest forth Thy Spirit, they were created: and Thou renewest the face of the earth.

Psalm 104:30

The Holy Spirit was actively involved in the creation of this world. He was one who created. He is able to bring forth something out of nothing. He can provide whatever we need.

2.   The Virgin Birth (Luke 1:35).

And the angel answered and said unto her, The Holy Ghost shall come upon thee, and the power of the Highest shall overshadow thee: therefore also that holy thing which shall be born of thee shall be called the Son of God.   Luke 1:35

The Holy Spirit was involved in actualizing the virgin birth. He miraculously came *upon* the Virgin Mary and caused her to conceive. The laws of nature do not bind the Holy Spirit.

3.   Regeneration (John 3:3, 5-8).

Jesus answered, verily, verily, I say unto thee, Except a man be born of water and of the Spirit, he cannot enter into the kingdom of God.   John 3:5

The Holy Spirit moves *upon* us and gives us the spiritual new birth we need. It is that regeneration, by the Holy Spirit, which makes us children of God.

4.   Resurrection (Romans 8:11).

But if the Spirit of Him that raised up Jesus from the dead dwell in you, He that raised up Christ from the dead shall also quicken your mortal bodies by His Spirit that dwelleth in you.   Romans 8:11

The Holy Spirit was actively involved in the physical resurrection of Jesus Christ. He helped give life back to Christ's physical body. One day, He will also physically raise up all who are born again.

5.   Intercession (Romans 8:26).

Likewise the Spirit also helpeth our infirmities: for we know not what we should pray for as we ought: but the Spirit itself maketh intercession for us with groanings which cannot be uttered.   Romans 8:26

The Holy Spirit is our Intercessor. He brings our prayers before God. We often do not know what to pray. He takes the prayers our lips can never properly verbalize and brings them eloquently before God. We do not have to worry about getting the words right.

6.   Testifying (John 15:26).

But when the Comforter is come, whom I will send unto you from the Father, even the Spirit of Truth, which proceedeth from the Father, He shall testify of me.
John 15:26

The Holy Spirit does not talk about Himself. When He ministers, He lets us and others, know about Jesus Christ.

One sure sign a work is not of the Holy Spirit is if it talks about the Holy Spirit more than about the Father or Jesus.

7. Giving Ministries (Acts 20:28).

Take heed therefore unto yourselves, and to all the flock, over the which the Holy Ghost hath made you overseers, to feed the church of God, which He hath purchased with His own blood.   Acts 20:28

The Holy Spirit gives each believer a *ministry* where we can serve God. We must realize the importance of our *ministry*. It is something God wants us to do.

8. Guiding (John 16:13).

Howbeit when He, the Spirit of Truth, is come, He will guide you into all truth: for He shall not speak of Himself; but whatsoever He shall hear, that shall He speak: and He will shew you things to come.
                                                                John 16:13

Though the Holy Spirit *convicts* the world of the things they do wrong, He *guides* (leads) the believer into the things, which are right to do.

If we honestly seek God's will, the Holy Spirit will make it known to us.

9. Teaching (John 14:26).

But the Comforter, which is the Holy Ghost, whom the Father will send in my name, He shall teach you all things, and bring all things to your remembrance, whatsoever I have said unto you.   John 14:26

The Holy Spirit is the one who helps us understand spiritual truths. He is our teacher.

As we read, or hear the Word of God preached, He makes it come alive in our lives.

He also helps us remember spiritual truths when we need them.

10. **Coming Upon Man** (Numbers 24:2; Judges 11:29).

> And Balaam lifted up his eyes, and he saw Israel abiding in his tents according to their tribes; and the Spirit of God came upon him. Numbers 24:2

The Holy Spirit does not have to use other agents or a go between to do His work with us. He ministers personally to, and through, man by personally coming *upon* us.

If someone claims he or she is God's special representative because they have more of the Holy Spirit *upon* them, than others do, they are deceived or are a deceiver. The Holy Spirit is a person, not some liquid you receive in portions. Either you have the Holy Spirit *upon* you or you do not.

11. **Inspiration** (2 Samuel 23:1-2; 2 Timothy 3:16; 2 Peter 1:19-21).

> All scripture is given by inspiration of God, and is profitable for doctrine, for reproof, for correction, for instruction in righteousness. 2 Timothy 3:16

> For the prophesy came not in old time by the will of man: but holy men of God spake as they were moved by the Holy Ghost. 2 Peter 1:21

The Holy Spirit moved *upon* godly men to give them the words God wanted for us. They recorded those words and those words became our Bible. The Bible is not just words, it is the actual Word of God to man.

12. **Filling Christ** (Luke 4:1-2).

> And Jesus being full of the Holy Ghost returned from Jordan, and was led by the Spirit into the wilderness. Luke 4:1

While Jesus ministered on earth, during His earthly ministry, He did not do it in His own power. He laid aside His own power and ministered through the power of the Holy Spirit. That same power is available to us.

13. Filling Believers (Ephesians 5:18).

And be not drunk with wine, wherein is excess; but be filled with the Spirit.   Ephesians 5:18

The Holy Spirit wants to *fill* believers. He wants to give them His power so they can live a godly life and have effective daily relationships with others.

14. Miracles of Christ (Matthew 12:28).

But if I cast out devils by the Spirit of God, then the kingdom of God is come unto you.   Matthew 12:28

The miracles Jesus accomplished, He did in the power of the Holy Spirit. God can provide us with that same power, when needed today, if He so chooses.

15. Glorifying Christ (John 16:14).

He shall glorify me: for He shall receive of mine, and shall shew it unto you.   John 16:14

The Holy Spirit does not lift up Himself. He lifts up Christ, so Christ is glorified. Just as Christ glorified the Father, the Holy Spirit glorifies the Son.

When we allow Him to work in our lives, we will glorify the Son.

16. Convicts the World (John 16:8-11).

And when He is come, He will reprove [convict] the world of sin, and of righteousness, and of judgment: of sin, because they believe not on me; of righteousness, because I go to my Father, and ye see me no more; of judgment, because the prince of this world is judged.
John 16:8-11

To *reprove (convict)*, means to pronounce guilty. This verse says the Holy Spirit convicts the *world*. The term *world* refers to the unsaved. The Holy Spirit identifies their wrong and causes them to feel guilty. On the other hand, the Holy Spirit wants to *lead* the Christian, He does not want to have to treat them like the world and *convict* them.

17.   Restrains Evil (2 Thessalonians 2:7).

> For the mystery of iniquity doth already work: only He who now letteth *[restrains]* will let *[restrain]* until He be taken out of the way.   2 Thessalonians 2:7

Though there is great wickedness on the earth, it would be much worse if it were not for the Holy Spirit and his restraining work. He keeps evil from having free reign.

This passage also teaches us one day the Holy Spirit will stop restraining sin on this world. That will occur during the Tribulation.

18.   Indwells the Believer (1 Corinthians 6:19; John 3:6-7).

> What? Know ye not that your body is the temple of the Holy Ghost which is in you, which ye have of God, and ye are not your own?   1 Corinthians 6:19

This passage addresses individual believers. Notice the shift from *ye (the second plural)* to the use of *you (the second person singular)*. God lives within the believer, individually, through the person of the Holy Spirit.

What a wonderful truth! We do not need a special consecrated building to meet with God. Our bodies are His temple. He lives within each one who is saved.

19.   Indwells the Church (1 Corinthians 3:16).

> Know ye not that ye are the temple of God, and that the Spirit of God dwelleth in you?   1 Corinthians 3:16

This passage addresses the church. Notice the double use of *ye,* the second person plural.

The Holy Spirit indwells each believer individually, but He also indwells a group of believers as a church, in a special way. We can never experience this fullness apart from His church.

20.   Seals the Believer (2 Corinthians 1:21-22).

> Now He which stablisheth us with you in Christ, and hath

anointed us, is God. Who hath also sealed us, and given us the earnest of the Spirit in our hearts.

2 Corinthians 1:21-22

The Holy Spirit puts God's seal *upon* us and clearly identifies each believer as belonging to God. There is no question about it, now and forever, once you are Christ's you are sealed and safely identified as His for all eternity.

21. Produces Fruit in Those Who Are Filled (Galatians 5:22-23).

But the fruit of the Spirit is love, joy, peace, longsuffering, gentleness, goodness, faith, meekness, temperance: against such there is no law.

Galatians 5:22-23

When we allow the Holy Spirit to fill *(control)* us, He produces fruit in our lives. A tree produces fruit for others, not for itself. The same is true of a fruitful Christ follower. That spiritual fruit the Holy Spirit produces in us is not for us, it is something He intends others to benefit from.

22. Renews (Titus 3:5).

Not by works of righteousness which we have done, but according to His mercy He saved us, by the washing of regeneration, and renewing of the Holy Ghost.

Titus 3:5

The Holy Spirit does away with all our old dead works when He saves us. He also makes us new in Christ. What a joy to have the renewing of the Holy Spirit. Through Him we become new creations in Christ (2 Corinthians 5:17).

23. Strengthens (Ephesians 3:16).

That He would grant you, according to His riches of glory, to be strengthened with might by His Spirit in the inner man. Ephesians 3:16

The Holy Spirit can give us all the strength we need to face each day and to live the abundant Christian life. Our own strength will fail us, but with the Holy Spirit, we have an incredible resource of unlimited strength.

24.   Sanctifies (1 Peter 1:2).

Elect according to the foreknowledge of God the Father, through sanctification of the Spirit, unto obedience and sprinkling of the blood of Jesus Christ: Grace unto you, and peace, be multiplied.   1 Peter 1:2

The word, *sanctify*, means, *to set apart for a specific purpose*. The Holy Spirit sets believers apart from this world *(sanctifies us)*, to be part of God's kingdom. This gives us a special position and purpose with multiplied grace and peace.

25.   Provides (Philippians 1:19).

For I know that this shall turn to my salvation through your prayer, and the supply of the Spirit of Jesus Christ.
                                                     Philippians 1:19

Christ uses the Holy Spirit to provide all our needs, both spiritually and physically. He can do this in quiet or in obvious ways. He can meet any need we have.

26.   Gives Gifts (1 Corinthians 12:1-6; Romans 12:6-8).

Now there are diversities of gifts, but the same Spirit.
                                                     1 Corinthians 12:4

Besides giving us salvation and meeting all our needs, the Holy Spirit gives everyone a *spiritual gift*. That *gift* gives us a unique *perspective* on life and the *potential* for spiritual service.

27.   Enlightens (1 Corinthians 2:9-14).

But God hath revealed them unto us by His Spirit: for the Spirit searcheth all things, yea, the deep things of God.   1 Corinthians 2:10

We are finite human beings with limited perception and comprehension, especially of spiritual matters and things we cannot see. The Holy Spirit enables us to understand what we need to know, especially spiritual truths, even very complex ones.

Dr. Larry A. Maxwell

Conclusion

In this chapter, we have seen the overwhelming evidence showing the Holy Spirit is God. We saw many of His attributes, looked at some of the names used to identify Him in the Bible, saw some of the symbols which refer to Him and took a brief look at some of His works. You must admit, He is truly wonderful.

As we continue this study, we will take a closer look at the Holy Spirit and the dynamic ways in which He relates to man.

50

CHAPTER TWO
QUESTIONS

Verses to Memorize: John 14:16-17

2.1   What do we mean when we say God is a Trinity?

2.2   How do we know the Holy Spirit is God?

2.3   What are some of the Attributes of the Holy Spirit?

2.4   What are some of the Names used in the Bible for the Holy Spirit and what is their significance?

2.5   What are the Symbols used in the Bible for the Holy Spirit? What do they teach us about the Holy Spirit?

2.6   What are some of the works of the Holy Spirit, which are especially meaningful to you?

QUESTIONS FOR ADDITIONAL THOUGHT

2.7   How does Deuteronomy 6:4, reinforce the teaching God is a Triune God?

2.8   Give a character sketch of the Holy Spirit based on His Names, the Symbols used for Him, and His works.

Dr. Larry A. Maxwell

CHAPTER THREE

The Holy Spirit in the Old Testament

The Distinction Between
The Old & New Testaments

Before we look at the work of the Holy Spirit in the Old Testament, it is important to identify when the Old Testament period ended and the New Testament period began. By that, I do not mean what is the last verse in the Old Testament and what is the first verse in the New Testament. What we need to distinguish is when did the New Testament relationship *(New Covenant)* begin between God and His people?

Though the section of the Bible entitled, *The New Testament,* begins with the Gospel of Matthew, chapter one, verse one, the New Testament relationship between God and His people did not begin until later in the book. Most of what happened in each of the Gospels occurred under *The Old Testament* economy. The New Testament relationship was not instituted until the death, burial and resurrection of Jesus Christ (1 Corinthians 15:1-11; Hebrews 9:11-15; Matthew 26:28). That is very important to understand.

> For I delivered unto you first of all that which I also received, how that Christ died for our sins according to the scriptures; and that He was buried, and that He rose again the third day according to the scriptures.
> 1 Corinthians 15:3-4

> How much more shall the blood of Christ, who through the eternal Spirit offered Himself without spot to God, purge your conscience from dead works to serve the living God? And for this cause He is the mediator of the new testament, that by means of death, for the redemption of the transgressions that were under the first testament, they which are called might receive the promise of eternal inheritance.
> Hebrews 9:14-15

Until the point the New Testament went into effect, the world was under the Old Testament economy. The cross is the focal point. Prior to the cross, God's people *looked forward* to the cross for salvation. Man lived under God's Law as their guide for life. The law did not *provide* salvation but *pointed to* salvation. It acted as a schoolmaster to provide guidelines for God's people to live under.

> Wherefore the law was our schoolmaster to bring us unto Christ, that we might be justified by faith. But after that faith is come, we are no longer under a school-master. For ye are all the children of God by faith in Christ Jesus.
> Galatians 3:24-26

Though people were saved in the Old Testament, it was not until after the death, burial and resurrection of Christ that man could receive the *Indwelling of the Holy Spirit* (John 7:39; 14:16-17; 20:22).

> But this spake He of the Spirit, which they that believe on Him should receive: for the Holy Ghost was not yet given; because that Jesus was not yet glorified.
> John 7:39

> And I will pray the Father, and He shall give you another Comforter, that he may abide with you for ever; even the Spirit of Truth; whom the world cannot receive. because it seeth Him not, neither knoweth Him: but ye know Him; for He dwelleth with you, and shall be in you.
> John 14:16-17

In the Old Testament, the Holy Spirit was *with* believers, but did not *indwell* them. The Holy Spirit could not *indwell* anyone until Christ shed His sinless blood, died for our sins, and was glorified.

Though the Holy Spirit did not permanently *indwell* man in the Old Testament, He was very active.

The Holy Spirit and Creation

The Holy Spirit was active before our world came into existence. In relation to His role with man, we find the Holy Spirit was actively involved in Creation.

O   The Hebrew plural word for God, ***Elohim***, is used in the Creation Account (*Genesis 1:1 and throughout the chapter*).

In the beginning God *[Elohim]* created the heaven and the earth.   Genesis 1:1

O   The plural terms, *Us,* and *Our,* are used by God, in the Creation Account. This is the Trinity speaking among themselves.

And God said, Let **Us** make man in **Our** image, after **Our** likeness...   Genesis 1:26a

And the LORD God said, Behold, the man is become as one of **Us**, to know good and evil...   Genesis 3:22

Some critics of the Biblical doctrine of the Trinity, say *us,* and *our,* in this passage, refers to God and His angels. There is not a single instance in the Bible where Angels are ascribed equality with God or any creative powers. Angels are created beings, they are not creators, and are never referred to by God as *us.*

For by Him were all things created, that are in heaven, and that are in earth, visible and invisible, whether they be thrones, or dominions, or principalities, or powers: all things were created by Him, and for Him: And He is before all things and by Him all things consist.
                                              Colossians 1:16-17

O   Direct Reference is made to the Holy Spirit in the Creation account and in other passages which speak of creation (Genesis 1:2; Job 26:13; 33:4; Psalms 33:6; 104:29-30; Isaiah 40:13).

The Holy Spirit brought both *form* and *life* to the new creation.

And the earth was without form, and void; and darkness was upon the face of the deep. And the Spirit of God moved upon the face of the waters.
                                              Genesis 1:2

The Spirit of God hath made me, and the breath of the Almighty hath given me life.   Job 33:4

The Holy Spirit and the World

The Holy Spirit does not exclusively minister to God's people. He has a ministry to all people, both saved and unsaved, in both the Old and New Testaments.

One of the roles of the Holy Spirit is to restrain sin (2 Thessalonians 2:7). This appears to have been one of His main works in the Old Testament.

> For the mystery of iniquity doth already work: only He who letteth *[restrains]* will let *[restrain]*, until He be taken out of the way.   2 Thessalonians 2:7

O   The Holy Spirit worked to restrain sin, and preserve mankind, in the days of Noah.

> And the LORD said, My Spirit shall not always strive *[duwn]* with man...   Genesis 6:3

In this verse, *strive* is the Hebrew word **duwn**, it means *to plead*. The Holy Spirit plead with mankind, trying to convince them, they were sinful and needed God.

Noah appears to have preached to these people, in the *power* of the Spirit, but no one other than his family responded (2 Peter 2:5).

O   The Holy Spirit is so powerful he stood firm and worked as a restraining influence against Satan himself.

> So shall they fear the name of the LORD from the west, and His glory from the rising of the sun. When the enemy shall come in like a flood, the Spirit of the LORD shall lift up a standard against him.
>   Isaiah 59:19

O   The Holy Spirit also worked actively in the affairs of nations to accomplish His plan (Isaiah 30:28-31).

> And His breath, as an overflowing stream, shall reach to the midst of the neck, to sift the nations with the sieve of vanity...   Isaiah 30:28a

The Holy Spirit and God's People

The way the Holy Spirit related to God's people in the Old Testament is significantly different from the way He relates to them in the New Testament.

Though God's presence was *with* His people, in the Old Testament, He could not permanently *indwell* them. The Holy Spirit could not permanently *indwell* man until the Messiah, Christ gave His life and shed His blood on the cross, as the perfect sacrifice for our sins (John 7:37-39; 14:16-17).

In Hebrews, the permanent *Indwelling of the Holy Spirit* is called, *the promise,* which the Old Testament believers were looking for.

> A new heart also will I give you, and a new spirit will I put within you: and I will take away the stony heart out of your flesh, and I will give you a heart of flesh. And I will put my Spirit within you, and cause you to walk in my statutes, and ye shall keep my judgments, and do them.   Ezekiel 36:26-27

> And these all, having obtained a good report through faith, received not the promise: God having provided some better thing for us, that they without us should not be made perfect.   Hebrews 11:39-40

Though the Holy Spirit could not *indwell* God's people in the Old Testament, He came *upon* some of them temporarily to *fill them with power* for a specific task.

The tailors who made Aaron's garments (Exodus 28:3) and the craftsmen who did the fine detailed construction for the Temple (Exodus 31:3) were all *filled* with the Spirit of God. They were filled with the *power* of the Holy Spirit for a specific task.

This was different from being *indwelled* by the Holy Spirit, or *filled* with the Spirit, in the New Testament. This parallels the New Testament teaching on the *Empowering by the Spirit.*

In most instances in the Old Testament, where the Holy Spirit worked directly in the lives of His people, the term **upon** was used.

The following are some of the people the Holy Spirit came *upon,* in the Old Testament, to *fill with His power* for a specific task:

1. The Seventy Elders (Numbers 11:16-17,25).

> And I will come down and talk with thee there: and I will take of my Spirit which is **upon** thee, and will put it **upon** them; and they shall bear the burden of the people with thee, that thou bear it not thyself alone.
>
> Numbers 11:17

God told Moses to choose seventy elders from among the children of Israel to help lead the people on their way from Egypt to the Promised Land. Those elders were to serve as judges between God's people, regarding civil matters. God gave them His wisdom and power, through the Holy Spirit, to help resolve conflicts, which arose among God's people.

2. Othniel (Judges 3:9-10).

> And the Spirit of the LORD came **upon** him, and he judged Israel, and went out to war... Judges 3:10a

Othniel was a judge and leader of Israel before Israel had kings. The Holy Spirit came *upon* him to help him lead God's people in battle.

3. Gideon (Judges 6:34).

> But the Spirit of the LORD came **upon** Gideon, and he blew a trumpet; and Abiezer was gathered after him.
>
> Judges 6:34

Gideon was another judge of Israel. The *power* of God came *upon* him to help him lead his people to victory.

4. Jephthah (Judges 11:29).

> Then the Spirit of the LORD came **upon** Jephthah, and he passed over Gilead and Manasseh...
>
> Judges 11:29a

Jephthah was another of Israel's judges God's *power* came *upon* for service.

5.   Samson (Judges 14:5-6).

...And behold, a young lion roared against him. And
the Spirit of the LORD came mightily **upon** him, and he
rent *[tore]* him as he would rent a kid...

Judges 14:6a

Samson was another of Israel's judges. At various times
in his life, the Holy Spirit came *upon* him in a mighty way.
Samson's incredible strength came from God, not from his
hair. His uncut hair was only a symbol of his commitment to
God.

6.   Saul (1 Samuel 10:6-10; 16:14).

But the Spirit of the LORD **departed** from Saul...

1 Samuel 16:14a

Saul was Israel's first king. The Holy Spirit came *upon*
Saul at different times. One day, because of Saul's
disobedience, the Holy Spirit departed never to return in the
same powerful way.

7.   David (1 Samuel 16:13).

Then Samuel took the horn of oil, and anointed him in
the midst of his brethren: and the Spirit of the LORD
came **upon** David from that day forward...

1 Samuel 16:13a

David, Israel's second king, had the Holy Spirit come
upon him. As far as we can tell, David is the only king in the
Old Testament whom the Holy Spirit came *upon* in *power*
and stayed *upon* for an extended period or else continued to
come *upon*.

At one point, David prayed asking God not to take the
Holy Spirit from him.

Create in me a clean heart, O God; and renew a right
spirit within me. Cast me not away from thy presence;
and take not thy Holy Spirit from me. Restore to me the
joy of my salvation; and uphold me with Thy Free Spirit.
Psalm 51:10-12

Like all other Old Testament believers, David did not

have the *Indwelling of the Holy Spirit*. David was not saying he was afraid of losing his salvation but rather of losing the *power* of God, which he had as the Holy Spirit was *upon* him. He knew sin would remove the joy and the *power* of the Holy Spirit from his life. This is a timely passage and concern for us today.

Other Ways the Holy Spirit Worked On Behalf of God's People

Besides coming *upon* specific believers for service, in the Old Testament, the Holy Spirit worked on behalf of God's people in other ways. It is interesting to note when the Holy Spirit worked in the lives of His people, others noticed.

> And Pharaoh said unto his servants, can we find such a one as this, a man in whom the Spirit of God is?
>
> Genesis 41:38

The Holy Spirit is also recognized as both teaching and providing for God's people, during the 40 years in the wilderness.

> Thou gavest also thy good Spirit to instruct them, and withheldest not thy manna from their mouth, and gavest them water for their thirst. Nehemiah 9:20

Though the Holy Spirit did not permanently *indwell* God's people in the Old Testament, He did work in their lives to lead them. The problem was, they often rebelled against that leading (Isaiah 63:9-10). He responded to their rebellion by disciplining them and attempting to lead them back to the truth.

> In all their affliction He was afflicted, and the angel of His presence saved them: in His love and in His pity He redeemed them; and He bare them, and carried them all the days of old. But they rebelled, and vexed his Holy Spirit: therefore He was turned to be their enemy, and He fought against them.
>
> Isaiah 63:9-10

Conclusion

As we have seen in this chapter, the Holy Spirit did not suddenly appear in the New Testament. He was very active throughout the Old Testament. He was active in creation, in the lives of the unsaved and in the lives of God's people.

His ministry to believers in the Old Testament was different from in the New Testament. Old Testament believers did not have the *Indwelling of the Holy Spirit*. At times, the Holy Spirit sovereignly came *upon* them and *filled* them with *power* for spiritual service. He departed when the task was accomplished.

In the next chapter, we will see another way the Holy Spirit worked in the lives of some believers in the Old Testament. It was He, who moved *upon* Holy Men to give us the Word of God, through inspiration and revelation.

CHAPTER THREE
QUESTIONS

Verses to Memorize: Genesis 1:1-2

3.1   What is the main difference between the Old and New Testament? When did the New Testament actually begin?

3.2   How do we know the Holy Spirit was actively involved in Creation?

3.3   How did the Holy Spirit work in relationship to the unsaved world in the Old Testament?

3.4   How did the Holy Spirit work in relationship to His people in the Old Testament? What could He not do for His people in the Old Testament that He does for all His people in the New Testament? Why?

3.5   Discuss David's concern in Psalm 51, about losing the Holy Spirit.

QUESTIONS FOR ADDITIONAL THOUGHT

3.6   What are the implications of the term *us,* in Genesis 1:26 and 3:22?

3.7   Give a profile of the work of the Holy Spirit in the Old Testament.

CHAPTER FOUR

The Holy Spirit and Revelation & Inspiration

The Foundation of Revelation & Inspiration

What a person believes about revelation and inspiration determines the rest of their theology. I know that is a strong statement, but it is true and very important to understand. Revelation and inspiration are foundational doctrines. They are the basis of how God communicates His *will* and His *word*, to mankind.

There is a lot of controversy regarding revelation and inspiration. Controversy in this area is especially strong between Liberal and Conservative theologians. Yet, it is interesting to note there is even controversy within the Liberal and Conservative camps over the nature and scope of what they believe about revelation and inspiration.

Many theologians believe the sixty-six books of the Holy Bible contain God's complete revelation to man. Those who believe that, differ in some important areas from those who believe God still reveals His authoritative word to mankind apart from the Bible.

There are those, such as I, who believe God verbally inspired the writers of the Holy Scriptures, in such a way that the Bible they wrote contains not only the Word of God to man but *God's very words*.

That differs significantly from those who believe the writers of the Bible were inspired, in the same way an artist or musician is inspired. They believe the final product of that inspiration is more human than godly. They believe the Word of God can therefore be flawed or subject to various interpretations. This leads to significantly differing views on doctrine.

It is not much use trying to reconcile different beliefs about various doctrines, especially about the work of the Holy Spirit, until you resolve the issue of what one believes about revelation and inspiration.

Definition of Revelation & Inspiration

It is important to understand the difference between revelation and inspiration. Most theologians agree with the following general definitions:

O **Revelation** - is the process by which God *reveals* His word to mankind.

O **Inspiration** - is the process by which man *receives* and *records* the revealed Word of God.

Revelation is solely an activity of God. Inspiration is an activity of God, using man as an *agent*. Those statements are where the agreement ends between the different schools of thought on revelation and inspiration.

The Biblical definition of revelation and inspiration is found in 2 Timothy 3:16-17 and 2 Peter 1:20-21.

> All scripture is given by inspiration of God, and is profitable for doctrine, for reproof, for correction, for instruction in righteousness: That the man of God maybe perfect, throughly furnished unto all good works.
> 2 Timothy 3:16-17

The word *inspiration* is the translation of the Greek word, **theopneustos**. It means, *God-breathed*. This is the only occurrence of this word in the New Testament.

There are two root words in **theopneustos**:

O **theo** - which means *God*, and

O **pneustos** - which comes from the word **pneuma**, which means *breath, wind or spirit*, as in the Holy *Spirit*.

The Old Testament word for *inspiration*, which is parallel to the Greek word **theopneustos,** is the Hebrew word, **neshamah**, found in Job 32:8.

> But there is a spirit in man: and the inspiration
> *[neshamah]* of the Almighty giveth them understanding.
>
> Job 32:8

The Holy Spirit is an essential part of revelation and inspiration. God inspired men to give us His word. Notice the emphasis in the following passage is upon the message from God.

> Knowing this first, that no prophecy of the scripture is of
> any private interpretation. For the prophecy came not in
> old time by the will of man: but holy men of God spake
> as they were moved by the Holy Ghost.
>
> 2 Peter 1:20-21

That passage tells us the Holy Spirit moved *(inspired)* man to record God's revelation, so the final product is God's recorded Word, bearing God's authority. God *breathed* the words and *guided* the men, as they wrote what He wanted written, so man could have God's Word. Though the Scriptures are clear on this, theologians differ as to the nature and scope of that revelation and inspiration.

Differing Views of Revelation & Inspiration

There are very distinct schools of thought regarding revelation and inspiration. Understanding this can help you understand why people can mean something very different from what you believe when they say the Bible is inspired.

A person's view regarding inspiration strongly affects their interpretation of the Scriptures.

1.   Liberal Views

The Liberal view accepts the teaching of Higher Criticism. Conservative theologians view this, as a destructive teaching because it concludes the Bible is an imperfect book.

This school of thought believes the Bible *contains* the Word of God, along with the words of man.

Those who hold to the Liberal view of inspiration and

revelation dispute the fact that Bible is inerrant (*the teaching that the Bible is without error*) and infallible (*the teaching that the Bible always works*).

There are two basic Liberal views regarding inspiration, those are the *Illumination View* and the *Intuition View*.

○ **Illumination View:**
Right Wing Liberal.

Those who hold the Illumination View do not believe the Bible *is* the Word of God. They believe various portions of the Scriptures *contain* God's revelation to mankind, while other portions do not.

To them, the question of which portions contain that revelation and which do not is disputable.

Those who hold this view believe some of the men who wrote the Bible were *illuminated* by God to perceive spiritual truths and these are recorded in certain portions of the Bible.

○ **Intuition View:**
Left Wing Liberal.

Those who hold the Intuition View do not believe the Bible *is* the Word of God. They believe the writers of the Scriptures had heightened natural religious *insight* from time to time and discovered spiritual truths, which they recorded.

Those who hold this view believe *some portions* of the Scripture show more insight than other portions. They believe some portions of the Scriptures should be disregarded. They accept *human intuition* rather than divine inspiration.

2. Neo-Orthodox Views

Neo-orthodoxy, sometimes known as *New Reformation* theology, accepts a Bible, which in their understanding, *becomes* the Word of God. This falls between the Liberal and Conservative views.

Those who hold this view believe the Bible *contains errors* but God uses this imperfect channel to confront man with His perfect word.

There are two basic Neo-Orthodox views regarding Inspiration, the *Existential View* and the *Demythologizing View*.

○ **Existential View:**
   Right Wing Neo-Orthodox.

   Men like Karl Barth and Emil Brunner, were Neo-Orthodox theologians who held to this view of inspiration. They taught God reveals Himself to mankind, through His Word, by means of personal encounters or crisis experiences.

   According to this view, when the words of the Scripture take on a *moment of meaning,* to an individual, and come alive, at that point, the Bible *becomes* the Word of God to that individual.

   Those who hold this view believe different passages *become* the Word of God at different times, to different individuals.

   A number of twentieth century church movements have held this view of inspiration.

○ **Demythologizing View:**
   Left Wing Neo-Orthodox

   Men like Rudolf Bultmann and Shubert Ogden, were Neo-Orthodox theologians who held to the Demythologizing view of inspiration. They taught God's word can be *found* in the Bible, if one can strip it of its' religious myths and cultural influences.

   Those who hold to this viewpoint will strip most of the miracles from the Bible.

3. Conservative Views

Conservative theologians believe the Bible *is* the very Word of God. They believe God wrote it and continues to speak to man through it.

There are three basic Conservative views regarding Inspiration, they are the *Verbal Dictation View*, the *Inspired Concept View* and the *Verbal Plenary Inspiration View*.

○ **Verbal Dictation View**:
   Right Wing Conservatives

   Those who hold to the Verbal Dictation View believe *every word* in the Bible was given to man by God in a *dictation* type fashion, as God did with Moses on Mount Sinai (Exodus 24:4; 34:27).

   Opponents often call these, *Mechanical Inspirationists*.

○ **Inspired Concept**:
   Left Wing Conservatives

   Those who hold to the Inspired Concept View believe God inspired the *thought* but allowed the writers to express it in *their own words*, the finished product bearing God's stamp of approval, hence being the Word of God.

   Those who hold this view believe God used the personalities of the writers to produce a Bible with varying styles. The focus is on the *concepts and thoughts* are God's Word , not *the actual words*.

   This is also called the *Dynamic View*. The Introduction to the *New International Version* of the Bible, explains this is the view of inspiration followed by its translators.

○ **Verbal Plenary Inspiration**:
   Conservative Consensus

   Those who hold to Verbal Plenary Inspiration believe all the *words* written in the Scriptures were *God-breathed*. They believe God gave full *(plenary)* expression to His thoughts by *guiding* the words of the writers, while using their personalities and backgrounds, to express His Word to man. Hence, the *very words* themselves are *the very words of God*.

I believe the Liberal and Neo-Orthodox teachings regarding revelation and inspiration are flawed. I whole-heartedly embrace the Conservative teaching on revelation and inspiration, specifically the Verbal-Plenary position. That position affects the rest of my theology. It also provides *a non-subjective standard* by which to measure the teaching of the Bible. That provides the greatest possible ground for unity among believers.

When we believe the words in the Bible, and their common accepted meanings at the time they were given, are the *very words* God wants us to have, we can understand more clearly the Word of God and have a strong basis for unity.

When people accept that teaching, and interpret the Bible literally in its grammatical and historical context, they cannot help but come up with a clear, non-subjective understanding of God's Word to man.

The Holy Spirit's Role in Revelation & Inspiration

The Holy Spirit has always revealed God and His word to mankind (2 Timothy 3:16-17; 2 Peter 1:20-21).

There have been distinct periods when the Holy Spirit did His work of Revelation and Inspiration in different ways:

1.   Before The Scriptures Were Written.

The events in the books of Genesis and Job, took place before any Scripture was written down. God revealed His Word to those patriarchs through the Holy Spirit (2 Peter 2:20-21).

2.   From The Time of Moses Until Christ.

Starting with Moses, God used both written Scripture, and His prophets, to reveal His Word to man. The following are some specific examples of how the Holy Spirit worded through individuals in the Old Testament to give mankind God's word.

○ **Moses** (Exodus 24:4; Numbers 14:22-23 cp. Hebrews 3:7-11).

Moses served as both a mouthpiece and pen for God. God used Moses to give us the first five books of the Bible.

○ **David** (2 Samuel 23:2; Many Psalms).

God used David as a pen. David penned the Word of God through many beautiful Psalms.

○ **Isaiah** (Isaiah 6:8-9 cp. Acts 28:25; Isaiah. 59:21).

God told Isaiah what to say to the people and had him record some of those words as the *very words of God*, which would be applicable to God's people throughout all ages.

○ **Jeremiah** (Jeremiah 1:4-9).

God called Jeremiah and began to use him when he was only a child.

God told him what to say and used him to write Lamentations and the Book of Jeremiah.

○ **Ezekiel** (Ezekiel 2:1-7).

The Holy Spirit came *upon* Ezekiel in *power*. God told Ezekiel to tell others God's words. God also used Ezekiel the write His words.

○ **Micah** (Micah 3:8).

God *filled* Micah with Holy Spirit *power*, so he could tell others God's Word.

○ **Other Prophets**.

God used other prophets as His mouthpieces throughout the Old Testament. He had some of them write down words He wanted us to have.

It is important to understand, not everything a prophet said was the Word of God. Only what they said when they were *moved by the Holy Spirit* was God's Word for the people they addressed.

It is also important to realize not everything a prophet said while being *moved by the Holy Spirit* was God's Word for *all* men. Sometimes those words were only for the immediate listeners. Hence, God did not have them record all their words. Various prophets wrote other books but did not ascribe God's authority to them.

What we have in the sixty-six books of the Old and New Testament are the complete Word of God to man. There is not any lost Scriptures God wanted us to have. The books claiming to be other Gospels were all written in the second century or later and are not authentic.

3. From The Time of Christ Until The Completion of The Bible.

Until the written Word of God was completed, God used previously written Scripture, some of the Apostles, as well as Paul, to reveal His Word to mankind.

○ **He Used Previous Written Scripture** (Matthew 4:4; Mark 1:2; Acts 1:20; Romans 1:17; 1 Corinthian 1:19; Colossians 4:16).

On occasions, God had people use previously written scripture, verifying its God given inspiration and authority.

○ **Peter** (Acts 2:14-40).

Peter spoke as God *filled* him with *power*. God also used Peter to give us the Epistles of First and Second Peter. He probably wrote much more, which was not Scripture.

○ **Stephen** (Acts 7:1-53).

Stephen spoke as God *filled* him with *power*. However, God did not have him write any Scripture.

○ **Paul** (Acts 13:16-41).

Paul spoke, referring often to the written Word of God. God also used him to write many of the books of the New Testament. He also wrote other books, which were not Scripture.

4.   From the Completion of The Bible.

The Book of Revelation was the last book God gave man, which contains His inspired words. That completed the Holy Spirit's work of inspiring and revealing God's words to mankind. What we have in the sixty-six books of the Holy Bible is God's complete revelation. (2 Timothy 3:16-17)

Though God still leads man today, those who proclaim God's Word must use the written Word of God as the basis of their message. It is the Scriptures alone, not the words of any man, which are inspired.

The Bible makes it clear, God's direct revelation of His words to man is only found today in His written Word. There is not any more direct revelation today, in the sense of carrying the authority of, *Thus saith the Lord* (Revelation 22:18-19).

Though God does not give us additional written or verbal revelation today, He uses the *Indwelling* of the Holy Spirit to *guide* His people, through the Word of God, in a *revealing way*, to help them make the correct application of His Word to their lives (John 14:26).

> Being born again, not of corruptible seed, but of incorruptible, by the Word of God, which liveth and abideth for ever.   1 Peter 1:23

The Bible is the *living Word of God*. As we read it and allow the Holy Spirit to bring it to life, it is as though God Himself is talking to us, but that is *not* revelation or inspiration. I find that to be one of the most wonderful aspects of the Christian life. Every day I can meet with God and know His words, as I open His Word.

> All Scripture is given by inspiration of God, and is profitable for doctrine, for reproof, for correction, for instruction in righteousness: that the man of God may be perfect, throughly furnished unto all good works.
> 2 Timothy 3:16-17

It is imperative we use the written Word of God in our preaching and in our presentation of the Gospel. The Holy Spirit strengthens the Christian's faith with His Word and convicts the lost with the completed written Word of God, so they can come to salvation (Romans 10:17; 1 Peter 1:23).

> So then faith cometh by hearing, and hearing by the
> Word of God.   Romans 12:17

The Preservation of The Word of God

God delivered His Word to Man and He preserves it. Throughout the ages, the Word of God has always endured and will continue to endure. When people made hand written copies, God made sure they copied them carefully.

Paul told Timothy he could be confident the *copies* of the Scriptures, which he had as a child *(for he had no originals)*, were the very inspired Word of God (2 Timothy 3:15-17).

> And from a child thou hast known the Holy Scriptures,
> which are able to make thee wise unto salvation through
> faith which is in Christ Jesus.
>   2 Timothy 2:15

Throughout the ages, some have sought to corrupt or destroy the Word of God. Some have produced corrupted translations, such as the *Jehovah's Witnesses*, with their *New World Translation*, but the Holy Spirit always preserves God's pure Word (2 Corinthians 2:17).

The Bible we have today, which is found in reliable translations which were based on a belief in verbal-plenary inspiration, such as the *Authorized Version (King James)*, are the very Word of God to man. They do not contain a mix of truth and error. We can confidently read such translations and know we have the Word of God.

> The words of the LORD are pure words: as silver tried
> in a furnace of earth, purified seven times. Thou shalt
> keep them, O LORD, Thou shalt preserve them from this
> generation for ever.   Psalm 12:6-7

73

Conclusion

A person's belief about revelation and inspiration are foundational to their entire outlook on the Scriptures and the Work of the Holy Spirit. The Bible is the complete Word of God to man.

Though the Holy Spirit no longer reveals God's Word to man, He helps convict the unsaved with His Word and leads believers to know God's will, through His Word.

The Holy Spirit is the key force behind the inspiration of Scripture. The key principle is the Holy Spirit came *upon* men in *power*, in such a way so they could deliver to us God's Words. They were delivered to us *by God* and have been preserved *by God* for us.

In the next chapter, we will look at the way the Holy Spirit worked in the Life of Christ.

CHAPTER FOUR
QUESTIONS

Verses to Memorize: 2 Timothy 3:16-17

4.1   Why is it important to understand what a person believes about Revelation and Inspiration?

4.2   What is Revelation?

4.3   What is Inspiration?

4.4   Summarize the Liberal view of Inspiration.

4.5   Summarize the Neo-Orthodox view of Inspiration.

4.6   Summarize the Conservative view of Inspiration.

4.7   What were the distinct periods and ways the Holy Spirit revealed God's Word to man?

4.8.   What did God mean when He said; He would preserve His Words for us?

QUESTIONS FOR ADDITIONAL THOUGHT

4.9   What is the significance of *theopneustos*?

4.10   Contrast the Conservative views of Inspiration.

Dr. Larry A. Maxwell

CHAPTER FIVE

The Holy Spirit and the Life of Christ

The Holy Spirit & Christ

Though a number of people are familiar with various aspects of the Holy Spirit's ministry with mankind, many are totally unaware of the incredibly significant role the Holy Spirit played in the life of Christ.

As you study the Scriptures, you can clearly see The Holy Spirit had a very active ministry in Christ's life. That ministry started with the incarnation *(His virgin birth)* and continued until the resurrection. This is a very dynamic truth, especially when you realize the same Holy Spirit, who worked in Christ's life, wants to work in your life.

To understand fully the Holy Spirit's role in the life of Christ, you need to understand the relationship between the members of the Trinity. Although all three are completely God and co-equal, they chose to submit themselves to each other in the roles they serve as they relate to man. The Father became the *Begetter* and the Son became the *Begotten.*

> And the Word [Jesus] was made flesh, and dwelt among us, (and we beheld His glory, the glory as the only begotten of the Father,) full of grace and truth.
>
> John 1:14

> For God so loved the world, that He gave His only begotten Son, that whosoever believeth in Him should not perish, but have everlasting life.
>
> John 3:16

The Holy Spirit's role in His ministry to man gave Him a unique relationship with the Father and the Son. The Father and Son became the *Sender* and the Holy Spirit became the one *Sent* to live inside of us.

> But the Comforter, which is the Holy Ghost, whom the Father will **send** in my name, He shall teach you all things...
>
> John 14:26a

There is another very important distinction to understand about the roles which the Trinity serve in relationship to man. The ministry of the Son always glorifies the Father (John 13:31-32; 14:13; 17:4) and the ministry of the Holy Spirit always glorifies Christ (John 16:13-14). Jesus spoke of the Father; the Spirit speaks to us of Christ.

> ...that will I do, that the Father may be glorified in the Son. John 14:13b

> Howbeit when He, the Spirit of Truth, is come, He will guide you into all truth: for He shall not speak of Himself; but whatsoever He shall hear, that shall He speak: and He will shew you things to come. He shall glorify me, for He shall receive of mine, and shall shew it unto you. John 16:13-14

Based on this distinction, one test of a ministry, which claims it is of God, is *does it speak more of Christ or of the Holy Spirit?* If it is of God, it will speak more of Christ.

Let us now look at some specific ways the Holy Spirit worked in the Life of Christ.

The Kenosis

One of the most significant ways the Holy Spirit was involved in the life of Christ was in relation to the *Kenosis*. *Kenosis* is a Greek word, found in Philippians 2:7. Many people are unfamiliar with this theological term. The *Kenosis* of Christ is something unique. It answers the following questions:

- ○ How did the Son of God become the Son of Man?

- ○ With Jesus being God, did He have an unfair advantage over sin and temptation while He lived on earth?

- ○ Did Jesus have all of His Godly powers to draw on during His earthly ministry?

- ○ If Jesus ministered through His Godly powers

how could we finite human beings ever hope to do anything eternally significant for God?

Those are valid questions about the Life of Christ, which find their answer in His relationship to the Holy Spirit.

The first answer to these questions is found in the doctrine of the *Kenosis*. Philippians 2:5-11 explains the *Kenosis*. It is the Biblical teaching that Christ voluntarily laid aside His Godly powers to be born, live and die, so He could fulfill redemption's work for us.

> Let this mind be in you, which was also in Christ Jesus: who, being in the form of God, thought it not robbery to be equal with God: but made Himself of no reputation, and took upon Him the form of a servant, and was made in the likeness of men: and being found in fashion as a man, he humbled Himself, and became obedient unto death, even the death of the cross.
>
> Philippians 2:5-8

Philippians 2:7, says He, *made Himself of no reputation*. That phrase is the translation of one Greek word, **kenosis**. *Kenosis* means to lay aside something intrinsic about one's self.

In the *Kenosis*, Jesus did not cease to be God, but He *laid aside* all His godly powers to become a man. He then lived and ministered in the *power* of the Holy Spirit. That brought us salvation and gives us hope.

> For He whom God hath sent [Jesus] speaketh the words of God: for God giveth not the Spirit by measure unto Him.
>
> John 3:34

When Christ came as the Son of Man, He did not minister in His own power as God. He voluntarily laid aside His own power as God and depended on the *power* of the Holy Spirit, as we too can depend on the Holy Spirit.

It was because Christ laid aside His godly powers He could experience what it was like to live as a human. He knows our pain, our joys, our struggles, our challenges and even the temptations we face, not just because of His omnipotence but because He personally experienced all those things and understands firsthand, what we are going through (Hebrews

2:14-18; 4:14-16). What a wonderful Savior!

> Forasmuch then as the children are partakers of flesh and blood, He also Himself likewise took part of the same; that through death He might destroy him that had the power of death, that is the devil; and deliver them who through fear of death were all their lifetime subject to bondage. For verily He took not on Him the nature of angels; but He took on Him the seed of Abraham. Wherefore in all things it behoved Him to be made like unto His brethren, that He might be a merciful and faithful high priest in things pertaining to God, to make reconciliation for the sins of the people. For in that He Himself hath suffered being tempted, He is able to succour *[help]* them that are tempted.
>
> Hebrews 2:14-18

The Virgin Birth

One of the most miraculous aspects of the Holy Spirit's ministry in the life of Christ was in the Virgin Birth. The Virgin Birth was the most miraculous, unique birth ever to occur. The Holy Spirit played a very important role in this special event.

God chose to become a man so He could live and die for all mankind. To become a man, He needed a mother. God chose a virgin, named Mary, to be the mother of Jesus (Luke 1:26-31; Isaiah 7:14).

> And in the sixth month the angel Gabriel was sent from God unto a city of Galilee, named Nazareth, to a virgin espoused to a man whose name was Joseph, of the house of David; and the virgin's name was Mary.
>
> Luke 1:26-27

God did not use two natural parents to bring Christ into this world because sin passes to the next generation through the man.

> For since by man came death, by man came also the resurrection of the dead. For as in Adam all die, even so in Christ shall all be made alive.
>
> 1 Corinthians 15:21-22

Any child, born of man, is born with both a sin nature and the condemnation of Adam's sin is on them (Romans 5:12-21).

> Wherefore, as by one man sin entered into the world, and death by sin; and so death passed upon all men, for that all have sinned.   Romans 5:12

To provide a Savior for man, who could bear man's sins, required a father who never sinned. To solve this problem, God Himself became the father (John 3:16; 2 Corinthians 5:21).

The fact the Holy Spirit was involved in the birth of Christ is not what made it unusual. The Holy Spirit is involved in each birth (Psalms 139:13-14).

> For Thou hast possessed my reins: Thou covered me in my mother's womb. I will praise Thee; for I am fearfully and wonderfully made: marvellous are Thy works; and that my soul knoweth right well.
>   Psalm 139:13-14

The Holy Spirit's role was unusual in the birth of Christ because with this birth, a human father was not involved (Luke 1:34-35; Matthew 1:18, 20-21).

The Holy Spirit miraculously came *upon* Mary and she conceived. With the help of the Holy Spirit, Jesus willingly became man for us (Hebrews 2:14). He was the only baby who ever chose to be born.

His Baptism

The Scripture mentions little regarding the childhood of Christ. During his childhood the Bible says He grew physically, socially and spiritually, as any other human could and should do (Luke 2:52; 1 Thessalonians 5:23).

> And Jesus increased in wisdom and stature, and in favour with God and man.   Luke 2:52

The earthly ministry of Christ did not begin until His baptism. It was there the Holy Spirit *came upon Him in power for service,* and remained *upon* Him (Mark 1:9-11; John 1:32-34).

> And it came to pass in those days, that Jesus came from Nazareth of Galilee, and was baptized of John in Jordan. And straightway coming up out of the water, He saw the heavens opened, and the Spirit like a dove descending upon Him; and there came a voice from heaven, saying, Thou art my beloved Son, in whom I am well pleased.
>
> Mark 1:9-11

At the baptism of Christ, the entire Trinity bore witness that this was the Son of God. *Jesus* bore witness with His presence, the *Father* bore witness with his verbal confirmation and the *Holy Spirit* bore witness by coming *upon* Christ.

The Apostle John, later tells us in 1 John, the Trinity bore witness to Christ both at His baptism *(water)*, and at His death *(blood)* (Matthew 3:16-17 cp. 1 John 5:6-8; John 19:34-35). John personally observed these two events.

> This is He that came by water and blood, even Jesus Christ; not by water only, but by water and blood. And it is the Spirit that beareth witness, because the Spirit is truth. For there are three that bear record in heaven, the Father, the Word and the Holy Ghost: and these three are one. And there are three that bear witness in earth, the Spirit and the water, and the blood: and these three agree in one.
>
> 1 John 5:6-8

Though Christ was undoubtedly *Indwelled* by the Holy Spirit from His birth, it was not until it was time for His ministry to begin, that the Holy Spirit came *upon* Him in *power* (Matthew 12:17-21 cp. Isaiah 42:1-4).

> Behold my Servant, whom I uphold; mine elect, in whom my soul delighteth; I have put my Spirit upon Him: He shall bring forth judgment to the Gentiles.
>
> Isaiah 42:1

Leading

Throughout the Life of Christ, we see His continued dependence on the Holy Spirit. Just as Christ depended on the Holy Spirit to lead Him, we need to depend on the Holy Spirit for His leading in our lives.

When Jesus was *Filled with the Power of the Holy Spirit*, He was *led* by the Holy Spirit (Luke 4:1; Acts 10:38).

> And Jesus being full of the Holy Ghost returned from Jordan, and was led by the Spirit into the wilderness.
>
> Luke 4:1

It was this **anointing** *(empowering)* of the Holy Spirit, which Christ chose as the means to enable Him to minister and make a difference in people's lives. He ministered in the *power* of the Holy Spirit.

> The Spirit of the Lord is upon me, because He hath **anointed** me to preach the gospel to the poor; He hath sent me to heal the brokenhearted, to preach deliverance to the captives, and recovering of sight to the blind, to set at liberty them that are bruised, to preach the acceptable year of the Lord.
>
> Luke 4:18-19

Jesus could have been born, lived a quiet sinless life and died for us. Our salvation would have been secured. But, He chose to live His life in the *power* of the Holy Spirit on a daily basis. He wanted us to see there is more to the Christian life than just accepting salvation and going to Heaven one day. There is a life of Spirit-filled service, awaiting each and every one of us, so we can point others to Christ and know the joy of bringing them to Heaven with us.

Teaching

Even Christ's teaching ministry, was done with the help of the Holy Spirit. Jesus could have taught everything Himself, but He allowed the Holy Spirit to work through Him in His teaching ministry.

> The former treatise have I made, O Theophilus, of all that Jesus began to do and teach, until the day in which He was taken up, after that He through the Holy Ghost had given commandments unto the apostles He had chosen.
>
> Acts 1:1-2

Jesus told the disciples in the Upper Room, the Holy Spirit is a teacher and would come later to teach His followers (John 14:26; 16:13). Today we have the Holy Spirit to help us as we seek to teach spiritual truths to others.

Miracles

The miracles of Christ were another aspect of His ministry which He could have done in His own power, but which He did in the *power* of the Holy Spirit.

Jesus healed the sick and the lepers. He made the blind see, the deaf hear, and the lame walk. He even raised the dead to life, all through the *power* of the Holy Spirit (Luke 4:18; Matthew 11:5).

Through the Holy Spirit, He claimed authority over demons and cast them out of those they were tormenting (Matthew 12:28; 9:32-33; Mark 1:5-20). He could have done this in His own *power* but He did it through the *power* of the Holy Spirit.

> If I cast out devils by the Spirit of God, then the kingdom of God is come unto you.   Matthew 12:28

Death

Even as Christ went to the cross, He depended on the Holy Spirit to help Him along the way (Hebrews 9:11-14). The Holy Spirit was with Him all the way *to* the cross, but *on* the cross Christ alone bore our sins and the grief of the world.

> How much more shall the blood of Christ, who through the Eternal Spirit offered Himself without spot to God, purge your conscience from dead works to serve the living God?   Hebrews 9:11

The Holy Spirit led Christ all the way to the cross where Christ willingly bore the sins of the world and completed the perfect offering for our sin.

As Christ hung on the cross, bearing the weight of our sins, God the Father turned His back on Him. Christ experienced separation from God the Father for the first time ever, all because he was bearing our sins. He cried out, *My God, my God, why hast Thou forsaken me?* (Matthew 27:46). This was in fulfillment of Psalm 22:1.

> My God, my God, Why hast Thou forsaken me? Why art Thou so far from helping me, and from the words of my roaring?   Psalm 22:1

Resurrection

From the beginning of Christ's life and ministry, all the way to His resurrection from the dead, the Holy Spirit played a pivotal role.

Christ willingly offered Himself a sacrifice for sin. He laid down His life for us and died alone. They took Him off the cross and buried Him in a borrowed tomb. Then, on the third day, death could not hold Him. With the help of the Holy Spirit, He was raised up, victorious over death (John 10:15-18; Romans 8:11; John 6:62-63).

> For Christ also hath once suffered for sins, the just for the unjust, that He might bring us to God, being put to death in the flesh, but quickened by the Spirit.
>   1 Peter 3:18

Through His death, burial and resurrection, Christ was glorified with the help of the Holy Spirit.

Now the Holy Spirit continues that work of glorifying Christ, by pointing people to the Savior, through us, as we minister in the *power* of the Holy Spirit (John 15:8).

> Now unto Him that is able to do exceeding abundantly above all that we ask or think, according to the power that worketh in us, unto Him be glory in the church by Christ Jesus throughout all ages, world without end.
>   Ephesians 3:20-21

Conclusion

We have seen in this chapter, the Holy Spirit was very active in the life of Christ. It was through the *power* of the Holy Spirit Jesus accomplished His ministry. That should be a real encouragement to us. The same Holy Spirit, who helped Christ, with every aspect of His earthly ministry, wants to help us live for Christ today. We do not have to do it alone!

In the next chapter, we will see how the Holy Spirit works in the life of the unsaved.

CHAPTER FIVE
QUESTIONS

Verses to Memorize: Philippians 2:5-8

5.1   What is one test, referring to the relationship between the Holy Spirit and Christ, which can be applied to see if a work which claims to be of God, really is?

5.2   What is the *Kenosis*, and what are its implications in your life?

5.3   What role did the Holy Spirit play in the Virgin Birth? Why was the Virgin Birth necessary?

5.4   What role did the Holy Spirit play at the baptism of Christ?

5.5   What other aspects of Christ's ministry were done in the *power* of the Holy Spirit?

5.6   What role did the Holy Spirit play in the death and resurrection of Christ?

QUESTIONS FOR ADDITIONAL THOUGHT

5.7   Explain the relationship among the Trinity, as seen in the roles they serve in relationship to man. Is any one member of the Trinity better, or more important, than the others?

5.8   What aspects of the Holy Spirit's work, in the life of Christ, can enhance your work and ministry for Christ?

Dr. Larry A. Maxwell

CHAPTER SIX

The Holy Spirit and the Unsaved

The Holy Spirit Has a Ministry to The Unsaved

Though the Holy Spirit plays a significant role in the lives of believers, the Holy Spirit also has a ministry to the unsaved. If it were not for the work of the Holy Spirit in the lives of the unsaved, no one would ever be saved.

There are different views regarding the nature and extent of the work of the Holy Spirit in the lives of the unsaved. Some believe He works the same in the lives of all people, offering everyone the same opportunity to become heirs of salvation. Others believe the Holy Spirit works only in a general way in the lives of all the unsaved and in a more specific way in the lives of a more limited group, whom they believe have been chosen for salvation. These issues are dealt with in more detail in the next chapter. Both schools of thought agree the Holy Spirit's ministry to the unsaved includes *Common Grace, Restraining Sin* and *Conviction*. We will look at each of those ministries.

Common Grace

One good definition for Grace is, *God giving us something positive, which we do not deserve.* Salvation is an act of grace. No one deserves to be saved.

Mercy is often coupled throughout Scripture with Grace. Mercy can be defined as, *God withholding from us something negative, which we do deserve.* We all deserve eternal separation from God because of our sins. It is the mercy of God, which withholds that punishment from us.

Common Grace is a specific category of grace. Common Grace can be defined as *the general work of the Holy Spirit, whereby God shows His grace on behalf of all men.* Notice from this definition, the beneficiary of this Common Grace is *all men.*

The Holy Spirit is the means God uses to impart this grace, to all men, for the common good of all men.

Everyone needs the Grace of God, both for salvation and for daily living. That grace is not something all men understand, it is only made clear through the work of the Holy Spirit (1 Corinthians 2:9-11).

> But as it is written, Eye hath not seen, nor ear heard, neither hath entered into the heart of man, the things which God hath prepared for them that love Him. But God hath revealed them unto us by His Spirit: for the Spirit searcheth all things, yea, the deep things of God.
>
> 1 Corinthians 2:9-10

God reveals Himself to all men, both *inwardly* and *outwardly*. Inwardly, He revels Himself through the working of the Holy Spirit on the heart of man. Outwardly, He revels Himself through his clear working in creation. Yet, in spite of all He does, men still choose to reject Him. Everyone makes their own choice and is responsible for it.

> For the wrath of God is revealed from heaven against all ungodliness and unrighteousness of men, who hold [*suppress*] the truth in unrighteousness; because that which may be known of God is manifest in them; for God hath showed it unto them. For the invisible things of Him from the creation of the world are clearly seen, being understood by the things that are made, even His eternal power and Godhead; so they are without excuse: Because that, when they knew God, they glorified Him not as God, neither were thankful; but became vain in their imaginations, and their foolish heart was darkened.
>
> Romans 1:18-21

We learn from Scripture, in both the Old and New Testaments, all men have the opportunity to see the grace of God, which brings salvation.

In the Old Testament account of the Genesis flood, we find the Holy Spirit actively working on behalf of mankind whose sins cried out to God (Genesis 6:3).

> And the LORD said, My Spirit shall not always strive with man, for that he also is flesh...   Genesis 6:3

The word *strive,* used in this verse, is the translation of the Hebrew word, **diyn**. In this context, it means, *to plead with someone*. God says, in this verse, the Holy Spirit pleads with man. This verse does not say it refers to some particular group of people, but to mankind as a whole. This verse includes the warning, one day that pleading ministry will stop.

In the New Testament, we see that same grace principle at work (Titus 2:11).

> For the grace of God that bringeth salvation hath appeared to all men.   Titus 2:11

In Paul's Epistle to Titus, God makes it clear this grace, *hath appeared to all men*, not to just some.

Some may wonder how all men everywhere could see the grace of God. The fact God says it is so should be enough. We can trust whatever He says.

There is another aspect to that which is important to remember. All people, no matter where they live on this earth, have godly ancestors who knew the personal saving grace of God. Noah is everyone's direct great grandfather. Noah and his sons knew God's way of salvation. As their descendants scattered throughout the world, they took that knowledge with them. As men abandoned their godly heritage some willfully abandoned their knowledge of the one true God and developed their own religious or non-religious systems (Romans 1:18-21). Even so, the Bible says, the grace of God continues to manifest itself to them.

Restraining Sin

Another work of the Holy Spirit, in relation to the unsaved, is restraining sin. When we look at all the sin around us, sometimes it may be hard to believe the Holy Spirit is restraining sin, but He is.

> For the mystery of iniquity doth already work: only He who now letteth *[katecho]* will let, until He be taken out of the way.   2 Thessalonians 2:7

91

The word, *letteth* **(katecho)**, is an old English word, which has almost the opposite meaning in modern English. It means *to restrain.* This passage tells us the Holy Spirit, on behalf of God's people, restrains the wickedness of man.

This verse indicates the Holy Spirit's ministry of restraining sin will continue until a specific time and will then cease. Many believe that takes place at the Rapture, when the church is removed from this world and the Antichrist is revealed. It appears during the Tribulation, man's sinfulness will be fully expressed without the Holy Spirit's restraining influence.

Some theologians, who do not believe in the Rapture, teach the binding of Satan took place after Christ's death on the cross. They say that aspect of the restraining work of the Holy Spirit is operating in the world today.

Dr. James M. Gray (1851-1935), a well-respected theologian commented on that interpretation sarcastically. He said, *If Satan is bound he must have a terribly long chain.* It is absurd some theologians believe Satan is bound with a long chain, making his binding irrelevant, and making the restraining work of the Holy Spirit, feeble at best. When God says Satan will be bound, that means he will be restrained, not tied to some long chain, which allows him to hurt people.

Sin is restrained during this present age, not because Satan is bound, but because of the Holy Spirit's restraining work. Satan is obviously loose and very active. He will be bound one day, but that will be during the millennial rule of Christ (Revelation 20:1-3).

Imagine how awful things will get on this planet without the restraining work of the Holy Spirit. It will truly be a time of tribulation.

Conviction

Another pivotal role the Holy Spirit has in relation to the unsaved is the role of convicting them.

> Nevertheless I tell you the truth; It is expedient for you
> that I go away: for if I go not away, the Comforter will

> not come unto you; but if I depart, I will send Him unto you. And when He is come, He will reprove [convict] the world of sin, and of righteousness, and of judgment: of sin, because they believe not on me; of righteousness, because I go to my Father, and ye see me no more; of judgment, because the prince of this world is judged.
>
> John 16:7-11

The word *reprove,* in this passage, is the translation of the Greek Word, *elegxei.* It means, *a trial in order to prove, to bring to light, to convince, to reprove, to convict.* In other words, the Holy Spirit puts man on trial. He does not put man on trial to see if man is lost or not. He puts man on trial to convince man, who is lost, of his lost sinful condition and need of a Savior.

In a sense, when we witness to others, about Christ, we are working for the prosecution in the courtroom of life. We must make a clear Biblical presentation of the facts. We must use the Word of God to show others they are guilty sinners whose sin has separated them from God. When we have done that, we can leave the convicting work up to the Holy Spirit, the chief prosecutor.

We must remember, we do not save anyone ourselves, we just do the witnessing; God is the one who does the saving. We are just the messengers He uses to bring His message to others.

1.   He Convicts the World of Sin (John 16:9).

Christ paid for the sins of the world on the cross.

> And He is the propitiation for our sins: and not for ours only, but also for the sins of the **whole world**.
>
> 1 John 2:2

The word *propitiation* means, *to satisfy a debt.* Christ satisfied God's righteous demand that sin must be punished. He paid the wages for sin, when He shed His precious blood and died on the cross. He died for the sins of the *whole world.* He paid the price for all our sins, in full.

No one goes to Hell just because of his or her sin; they perish because they will not place their belief in the finished work of Christ. Our unbelief condemns us.

For God sent not His Son into the world to condemn the world; but that the world through Him might be saved. He that believeth on Him is not condemned: but he that believeth not is condemned already, because he hath not believed in the name of the only begotten Son of God.

John 3:17-18

He that believeth on the Son hath everlasting life: and he that believeth not the Son shall not see life, but the wrath of God abideth on him.

John 3:36

The Holy Spirit convicts the unsaved of their lost sinful condition so they can see their need of the Savior and believe on the Lord Jesus Christ and be saved.

2. He Convicts the World of Righteousness
(John 16:10)

We are not only guilty of committing sin, but we are also guilty of not being righteous (Romans 3:10).

As it is written, There is none righteous, no not one.

Romans 3:10

One of the key aspects of righteousness is doing what is right in God's eyes. God is not only concerned about the wrong things we do, which we recognize as sin. God is also concerned about the right things we should do, but do not do. We are guilty before God because we do not do the good we should do. We are not righteous. We all fall short of the glory of God.

For all have sinned, and come short of the glory of God.

Romans 3:23

The resurrection and ascension of Christ prove He was righteous and His sacrifice for our sin was accepted. If He was not righteous, He could not have died for our sins. He would have died for His own sins and remained in the grave. Because He was righteous, He could die for our sins and then rise victoriously over death. No one else has ever done anything like that. It proves He is the only way to God and He alone can make us righteous (John 14:6; Romans 10:9-13).

Jesus saith unto him, I am the way, the truth, and the life: no man cometh unto the Father but by me.

John 14:6

That if thou shalt confess with thy mouth the Lord Jesus, and shalt believe in thine heart that God hath raised Him from the dead, thou shalt be saved. For with the heart man believeth unto righteousness; and with the mouth confession is made to salvation.

Romans 10:9-10

None of us is righteous enough to go to Heaven on our own. The Holy Spirit makes it clear we need God's righteousness in order to have a personal relationship with God.

3. He Convicts the World of Judgment
(John 16:11)

The Holy Spirit not only shows the world it is guilty of sin, and lacking in righteousness, He shows the world there is judgment for that sin and unrighteousness.

Christ was punished for our sins on the cross. Satan was defeated by Christ's death and his final judgment were sealed (Revelation 20:10; Matthew 25:41). All who will not place their faith in Christ, those who seek to serve themselves and knowingly or unknowingly follow the path of the prince of this world shall join him in perpetual separation from God for all eternity. The Holy Spirit seeks to make this clear to unsaved man.

And the devil that deceived them was cast into the lake of fire and brimstone, where the beast and the false prophet are, and shall be tormented day and night for ever and ever. And I saw a great white throne, and Him that sat on it, from whose face the earth and heaven fled away; and there was found no place for them. And I saw the dead, small and great, stand before God; and the books were opened: and another book was opened, which is the book of life: and the dead were judged out of those things which were written in the books, according to their works. And the sea gave up the dead which were in it; and death and hell delivered up the dead which were in them: and they were judged every man according to their works. And death and hell were cast into the lake of fire. This is the second death. And whosoever was not found written in the book of life was cast into the lake of fire.

Revelation 20:11-15

The Holy Spirit's ministry, in relation to the unsaved, is a convicting ministry. Some Christians continue in practices, which are not pleasing to the Lord and piously say they will stop what they are doing if the Lord *convicts* them. Christians should allow the Lord to *lead them* instead of waiting to *be convicted* like a guilty unsaved sinner.

Conclusion

We saw in this chapter the Holy Spirit works specifically in the lives of the unsaved. Though they may not recognize His working, He is active in their lives.

The Holy Spirit's main work in the lives of the unsaved is to convict them of sin, or righteousness and of judgment so they see they are lost sinners in need of a Savior.

In the next chapter, we will see the Holy Spirit brings us from our unsaved state to the place of salvation in Christ.

CHAPTER SIX
QUESTIONS

Verses to Memorize: John 16:7-11

6.1   What do most conservative theologians agree are the three works of the Holy Spirit on behalf of the unsaved?

6.2   What is the difference between Grace and Mercy?

6.3   What is Common Grace?

6.4   What is the restraining work of the Holy Spirit?

6.5   What are the three things the Holy Spirit convicts the world of today?

QUESTIONS FOR ADDITIONAL THOUGHT

6.6   What are the two ways the Holy Spirit makes Himself known to all men?

6.7   Why does the Holy Spirit convict the world of sin?

Dr. Larry A. Maxwell

CHAPTER SEVEN

The Holy Spirit and Salvation

Regeneration

One of the most wonderful things a person can ever have is a personal relationship with God. That relationship with God is one of the special benefits given to all who find salvation in Christ. The Holy Spirit has played, and continues to play, a very active role in that salvation. He was intimately involved in the life of Christ, from His birth to His resurrection. He worked in, through, and with Christ, making the provision for salvation possible.

Though the provision for salvation was made for all men, and though God is not willing any should perish (2 Peter 3:9), it is a sad truth all men will not be saved (Revelation 20:11-15).

The Bible makes it very clear no one can earn his or her salvation. Salvation is a gift from God (Romans 6:23). To be saved, a person must personally accept the gift of salvation in faith (Ephesians 2:8-9). That is where the Holy Spirit and regeneration come in.

Regeneration is the work of the Holy Spirit whereby He makes the unsaved sinner a *reborn child of God* (Titus 3:5; John 3:3-5; 1 Peter 1:23).

> Not by works of righteousness which we have done, but according to His mercy He saved us, by the washing of regeneration, and renewing of the Holy Ghost.
> Titus 3:5

> Jesus answered, Verily, verily I say unto thee, Except a man be born of water and of the Spirit, he cannot enter into the kingdom of God. That which is born of the flesh is flesh; and that which is born of the Spirit is spirit. Marvel not that I said unto thee, Ye must be born again.
> John 3:5-7

It would seem the regeneration of lost sinners by the Holy Spirit would be a very straightforward, non-controversial teaching, yet for years, this has been a main area of controversy among Christians. Theologians are divided over *how* the Holy Spirit accomplishes the work of regeneration, and over *who can* or *who will* be regenerated, as well as over the *nature* of that regeneration.

Calvinism & Arminianism

Among conservative Christians, *Calvinism* and *Arminianism* are the two main schools of thought on the issue of regeneration and the work of the Holy Spirit in relation to salvation. I will briefly address a third school of thought at the conclusion of this chapter, which is somewhere between *Calvinism* and *Arminianism.*

I grew up in a Baptist church, which was somewhat *Calvinistic* in its approach to salvation. I later learned not all Baptists believe that way. After I became involved in the *Jesus People* Movement *(Neo-Pentecostalism)*, I began my study for the ministry in the *Nazarene Church.* The *Nazarene Church* is *Arminian* in its approach to salvation. Though both churches held to the two different schools of thought regarding the work of the Holy Spirit in relation to salvation, I never heard the terms *Calvinism* or *Arminianism* until I went to Bible College.

The first night I was in Bible College, the upper classmen in my dorm tried to determine the doctrinal positions of the new students. The school I attended was founded at the turn of the twentieth century as a very strong evangelistic and conservative, non-denominational school. Not long before I arrived, some of the faculty began to teach a strong *Calvinistic* position relating to salvation. When the upper classmen heard I started my studies for the ministry in a Nazarene church, and that I had been part of the *Jesus People* movement, they quickly descended on me looking for a debate. The terms *Calvinism* and *Arminianism*, quickly became part of my understanding and vocabulary.

In my quest for the truth, I spent many hours researching both sides of the debate. I wanted to know how each started and wanted to understand what they believed. Too often people accept definitions of what different groups believe, from people outside those groups. That is *second hand information.* Usually the definitions one gives of their opponent's viewpoints are flawed. That can lead to a lot of misunderstanding. To get a proper understanding, I went back and researched the writings of the theologians who formulated the various positions. I also investigated church history and came up with the following discoveries.

Those who identify themselves as *Calvinists,* follow the teachings of John Calvin, a Catholic priest who converted to Christ in 1536, at the age of 26, during the Reformation in Switzerland.

After his personal conversion, Calvin taught a salvation by faith, wholly of grace. His teachings were at odds with the works based salvation theology, taught at that time by the Catholic Church. Through his study of the Scriptures, Calvin concluded man was so sinful he could never do anything to achieve salvation. He taught salvation could only be wrought in man by a special work of the Holy Spirit. In his understanding, the Holy Spirit irresistibly draws select individuals to God. Only through the Holy Spirit's enabling, can people place their faith in God and be born again. A believer, thus reborn by the work of the Holy Spirit, will live a holy life and faithfully persevere until Christ's return.

Calvin also taught the death of Christ on the cross, though *sufficient* for all humankind, was only *effective* for the elect who would accept that salvation. That teaching means Christ's death was *sufficient* to save the whole world but only *practically* saves the elect.

John Calvin's teachings were set forth in a series of books known as, *Calvin's Institutes.* His theology quickly spread and was adopted by many of the Reformation churches.

In 1609, the Netherlands *(Holland & Belgium)* separated from Catholic France. At that time the *Dutch Reformed Church,* which was *Calvinistic* in its theology, became the state church in the Netherlands.

In 1610, Jacob Arminius, a leading theologian at the time, wrote *The Remonstrance,* to set forth what he believed. His teachings conflicted with various beliefs held by the *Calvinists.* Arminius' strongest objection was to the *Calvinistic* teaching that God decreed specific individuals would be saved while all others would be lost. He and his followers drafted what became known as the *Five Points of Arminianism*, to counter the *Calvinistic* teaching.

The **Five Points of Arminianism** can be summarized as follows:

1. **God Elects or Reproves on the Basis of *Foreseen* Faith or Unbelief.**

2. **Christ Died for All Men and for Every Man, Although Only Believers Will Be Saved.**

3. **Man is So Depraved Divine Grace is Necessary Unto Faith or Any Good Deed.**

4. **This Grace May Be Resisted.**

5. **Whether All Who Are Truly Regenerate Will Certainly Persevere in the Faith, is a Point Which Needs Further Investigation.**

In 1618-1619, the Dutch Reformed Church, held the *Synod of Dort*, to review the differences between the *Calvinists* and *Arminianists*. As a result of that synod, the *Arminianists* were ousted by the church.

The *Five Points of Calvinism* were drafted, to counter the *Five Points of Arminianism* and summarize the *Calvinist's* position. The first letter of each of the *Five Points of Calvinism* spells out the word TULIP.

The **Five Points of Calvinism** are as follows:

1. **Total Inability/Total Depravity.**
   Man does not have the ability to be saved or to turn to God.

2. **Unconditional Election.**
   God has chosen an elect few to be the recipients of special grace and of eternal salvation.

3. **Limited Atonement/Particular Redemption.**
   Christ's work on the cross was to secure salvation only for the elect.

4. Irresistible Grace/ The Efficacious Call of the Spirit.
Man cannot resist the call of the Spirit. All the elect shall be saved.

5. Perseverance of the Saints.
Those who are truly the elect will persevere to the end.

The two issues in the *Calvinism* versus *Arminianism* debate, which primarily involve the work of the Holy Spirit, are *Irresistible Grace* and *Eternal Security*. The following briefly compares and contrasts what each side teaches on these two issues.

Irresistible Grace

Calvinism teaches the Holy Spirit draws a person to Christ. There are some *Arminianists* who believe that too. *Calvinism* goes further and says the drawing of the Holy Spirit is *exclusively* for a specific group known as *the elect* and such drawing cannot be resisted. *Arminianists*, who believe in this drawing of the Holy Spirit, believe it is for all men and can be resisted.

The *Calvinist's* position on Irresistible Grace, is explained clearly in, *Romans, An Interpretive Outline*, by David N. Steele and Curtis C. Thomas:

> *Although the general outward call of the gospel can be and often is, rejected, the special inward call of the spirit never fails to result in conversion of those to whom it is made. This special call is not made to all sinners but is issued to the elect only.*

If you would like to investigate this more thoroughly the following are verses used by *Calvinists* in their defense of Irresistible Grace: 1 Corinthians 2:10-14; 1 Peter 1:2; John 1:12-13; Titus 3:5-7; Ezekiel 36:23-28; Matthew 11:25-27; John 6:37, 44-45, 64-65; Ephesians 1:17-18; Acts 13:48; Ephesians 2:8-9; 2 Timothy 2:25-26; Galatians 1:15-16; Romans 9:11 and Romans 9:16.

Dr. John R. Rice, Fundamental evangelist and author of many books, expressed his concerns about the doctrine of *Irresistible Grace* in his book, *Predestined for Hell? No!*

> *By this term Calvin meant, and hyper-Calvinists today mean, that God intended for only a limited number of people to be saved, that the atonement of Christ paid for the sins of only the limited few (the doctrine of 'limited atonement', as extreme Calvinists call it) that those who are predestined to be saved cannot resist the grace of God, cannot reject the Savior but are certain to be saved. For this reason extreme Calvinists are not generally burdened about soul-winning since, they say, the grace of God is 'irresistible'.*

Verses used by theologians, who counter Irresistible Grace, include some of the same verses the *Calvinists* use to prove it, as well as Revelation 3:20; John 3:14-17; Romans 10:9-21; Matthew 23:37 and Revelation 22:17.

No matter which of these two positions you embrace, it is important to remember, we have a responsibility to present the Gospel to all mankind (Matthew 28:19-20; Mark 16:15; Romans 10:14-17). We are to present the Gospel the Holy Spirit will do the drawing.

Eternal Security

The next area of controversy between the *Calvinist* and *Arminianist*, involving the Holy Spirit, is the area of the security of the believer. Today, a person's belief regarding what is often called *Eternal Security*, is usually the main issue laymen use to identify themselves as a *Calvinist* or an *Arminianist*. There is much more to those two schools of interpretation than that one issue.

A person who believes they can lose their salvation is usually identified as an *Arminianist*. The one who believes you cannot lose your salvation is often called a *Calvinist*.

People who hold to the position you cannot lose your salvation are often said to believe in *Eternal Security*. It is important to understand there is a difference between *Eternal Security* and *Calvinism's* doctrine of *Perseverance of the Saints*.

True *Calvinists* prefer the term *Perseverance of the Saints*, over *Eternal Security*. *Calvinist* Theologian Charles Horne, explains why in his book, *Salvation*.

> *Perseverance is a much more adequate term than eternal security to describe the scriptural concept intended here. It is utterly wrong to say that a believer is quite secure irrespective of his subsequent life of sin and unfaithfulness. The truth is that the faith of Jesus Christ is always respective of the life of holiness and fidelity.*

The practical application of the *Calvinistic* teaching of *Perseverance of the Saints* and the *Arminian* teaching that people can lose their salvation are surprisingly *somewhat* similar.

The *Calvinist* believes a person, who attends church and appears to be part of the Body of Christ, but then turns away from the Lord and continues in sin, does not have salvation because that person was not a believer in the first place.

The *Arminianist* believes the person who was part of the fellowship but then departs to continue in sin, lost their salvation. Both parties believe the person, in their final state, is not saved.

The Eternal Security position actually falls somewhere between the *Calvinist* and *Arminian* teachings. Those who hold to the Eternal Security position usually believe the following:

1.   Salvation Depends on God, Not on Us.

For by grace are ye saved through faith; and that not of yourselves: it is the gift of God: not of works, lest any man should boast.

Ephesians 2:8-9

2.   Our Salvation is Eternally Secure Because God Does the Keeping (John 3:16; 10:27-30).

My sheep hear my voice, and I know them, and they follow me: and I give unto them eternal life; and they shall never perish, neither shall any man pluck them out of my hand. My Father, which gave them me, is greater than all; and no man is able to pluck them out of my Father's hand. I and my Father are one.

John 10:27-30

3. **Though Christians Do Not Have to Sin, It is Possible and Probable that Christians Can, and Will, Commit Almost Any Sin Imaginable.**

Such sin, no matter how horrible it may seem, does not cause one to lose their salvation, nor does it mean they were not saved to begin with (1 John 2:1; 1:9).

My little children, these things write I unto you, that ye sin not. And if any man sin, we have an advocate with the Father, Jesus Christ.

1 John 2:1

If we confess our sins, He is faithful and just to forgive our sins, and to cleanse us from all unrighteousness.

1 John 1:9

4. **It is Possible a Believer Who Sins, May Continue in That Sin Until They Die.**

This too does not cause them to lose their salvation, nor does it indicate they were never saved. However, most who hold to the teaching of Eternal Security believe if a believer continues in sin, God will deal with such a person, in His own time, according to the following three steps:

O **First, He will reprove them** (Proverbs 1:23; 6:23; Galatians 6:1).

Turn you at my reproof: behold, I will pour out my Spirit unto you, I will make my words known unto you. Proverbs 1:23

O **Next, if they do not respond, He will chastise (*discipline*) them** (Hebrews 12:3-17).

For whom the Lord loveth He chasteneth, and scourgeth every son He receiveth.

Hebrews 12:6

O **Finally, if they still will not respond, He will kill them** (Isaiah 22:12-14; 1 John 5:16).

And it was revealed in mine ears by the LORD of Hosts, Surely this iniquity shall not be purged from you till ye die, saith the Lord God of Hosts.   Isaiah 22:14

If any man see his brother sin a sin which is not unto death, he shall ask, and He shall give them life for them that sin not unto death. There is a sin unto death: I do not say that he shall pray for it.   1 John 5:16

5.   This View Strongly Believes Our *Actions* Do Not Determine If We Keep Or Lose Our Salvation.

Whether we persevere or not, whether we do anything or not, our salvation is eternally secure. Our actions do not determine our salvation, they determine our rewards (Romans 14:10; 1 Corinthians 3:10-15).

Every man's work shall be made manifest: for the day shall declare it, because it shall be revealed by fire; and the fire shall try every man's work of what sort it is. If any man's work abide which he hath built thereupon, he shall receive a reward. If any man's work shall be burned, he shall suffer loss: but he himself shall be saved; yet so as by fire.

1 Corinthians 3:13-15

A Third School of Thought

Today there are conservative Christians on both sides of the debate. There are those who hold to the *Calvinistic* school of thought and those who follow the *Arminian* school of thought. I learned there are also other conservative theologians who find their theology somewhere in between the teachings of these two groups. Some refer to them as ***Biblists***.

The 1828 Webster's Dictionary defined the word **Biblist**, as, *one who makes the Scriptures the sole rule of faith.*

Some theologians referred to as *Biblists* included Dr. Andrew Telford, author of *Subjects of Sovereignty*, J. Vernon McGee, W.A. Criswell, Jack Wyztzen, founder of *Word of Life*, Dr. Jerry Falwell, founder of *Liberty University* and Dr. John R. Rice, editor of *The Sword of the Lord.*

Though some **Biblists** are sometimes identified as *Calvinists*, they disagree strongly with the *Calvinist* doctrime of Limited Atonement. They also embrace the doctrine of Eternal Security instead of Perseverance of the Saints. As explained above, Eternal Security is not a *Calvinistic* teaching, nor is it an *Arminian* teaching.

Dr. Gary C. Woods in his *Guide to Theologians*, listed theologians who did not fully embrace Limited Atonement or Perseverance of the Saints. He called them *Mediate Theologians*. He surprised many by including Charles H. Spurgeon in his list. Spurgeon is often listed as a strong Calvinist, yet Woods showed Spurgeon taught both Limited and Unlimited Atonement. Woods list includes: Lewis Sperry Chafer, John F. Walvoord and Charles Ryrie, from Dallas Theological Seminary; David Jeremiah, Harold Wilmington, Josh McDowell and Rick Warren.

Both *Calvinists* and *Arminianists* believe they regard the Bible as their only rule of faith. Yet, Church Historian Philip Shaff (1819-1893), whom *Calvinists* claim as one of their own, in his *History of the Christian Church,* wrote:

> *Calvinism emphasizes divine sovereignty and free-grace; Arminianism emphasizes human responsibility. The one restricts saving grace to the elect, the other extends it to all men on the condition of faith. Both are right in what they assert; both are wrong in what they deny. If one important truth is pressed to the exclusion of another truth of equal importance, it becomes an error, and loses its hold upon conscience. The Bible gives us a theology, which is more human than Calvinism and more divine than Arminianism, and more Christian than either of them.*

Conclusion

It is important to remember there are good believers who sincerely hold differing viewpoints on how the Holy Spirit works in relation to salvation.

Those with opposing viewpoints are often very critical of any other viewpoint. It is true, both sides cannot be correct, but for some reason, both think they are.

Remember both sides teach salvation by grace, through faith. Though they differ strongly on this issue, if they are born again, they are still part of the family of God and must be treated as family members, not as the enemy.

No matter which view you hold, regarding salvation, whether *Calvinism, Arminianism*, or somewhere in-between, remember the Holy Spirit plays an active part in salvation.

In the remaining chapters in this book, we will see how the Holy Spirit works in the life of those who are saved.

CHAPTER SEVEN
QUESTIONS

Verse to Memorize: Titus 3:5

7.1 What is Regeneration?

7.2 What are the *Five Points of Arminianism*?

7.3 What are the *Five Points of Calvinism*?

7.4 What does Irresistible Grace mean?

7.5 Contrast Perseverance of the Saints and Eternal Security.

7.6 What is a Biblist? What do they believe?

QUESTIONS FOR ADDITIONAL DISCUSSION

7.6 Discuss Philip Shaff's statement regarding *Arminianism* and *Calvinism*.

7.7 Discuss John R. Rice's statement regarding Irresistible Grace.

CHAPTER EIGHT

The Holy Spirit and The Saved: The Indwelling

Understanding the Terminology

The Holy Spirit plays an absolutely vital role in the lives of those who accept Jesus Christ as their Lord and Savior. In this and the following chapters we will look at, the *Three-fold Work of the Holy Spirit* in the life of the believer.

As you undertake this study of the work of the Holy Spirit in the life of the believer, it is important to understand the definitions of the terms a person uses. Different Bible teachers use different terms to describe various aspects of the work of the Holy Spirit. Sometimes the same terms mean different things to different people. I found that very confusing when I first started this study more than forty years ago. I heard some people use the same words to describe the working of the Holy Spirit, but found out they meant different things. Then I heard other people use different words, which to me had quite different meanings, to describe the same work of the Holy Spirit. That was, and still is, a very real and confusing problem.

To avoid confusion or misunderstanding, it is important to understand what a person means when they use a particular word to refer to some aspect of the work of the Holy Spirit. Some people use the same words but mean entirely different things. For example, when R.A. Torrey, speaks of *receiving the Holy Spirit,* he is not talking about receiving the *Indwelling of the Holy Spirit*, which all believers receive at salvation. When Torrey uses those words, he is referring to receiving the *Empowering of the Holy Spirit* for service.

Some refer to receiving the *power of the Holy Spirit* for service as, the *Baptism of the Holy Spirit.* But, when John Walvoord, in his book, *The Holy Spirit*, speaks of the *Baptism of the Holy Spirit,* he is referring to the *Indwelling of the Holy Spirit*. You must make sure you understand what a person means by the terms they use.

Even the Word of God uses similar terms to describe the various works of the Holy Spirit in the life of the believer. It is important to determine the context of the passage, identify the various meanings of the words used, and carefully interpret Scripture by Scripture, in order to gain a proper understanding of what is being taught.

Another important principle to keep in mind, especially when discussing this issue is this; *you must interpret your experiences by the Word of God, rather than interpreting the Word of God by your experiences.*

Too many people have an experience, and then seek to justify it by Scripture. On the other hand, sometimes they allow their experience to bias their interpretation of the Word of God. Experience is not reliable, but the Word of God is.

> The heart is deceitful above all things, and desperately wicked: who can know it?   Jeremiah 17:9

That verse is addressed to God's people. Even though we are God's people, we can deceive ourselves. We cannot let our experiences guide us. Carefully examine any experience you have, with the light of the Word of God. You may discover what happened to you is not what you originally thought it was.

In this study, the words, the INDWELLING, the FILLING and the EMPOWERING, are used to describe the three major ways the Holy Spirit works in the lives of the believer. I refer to these as the *Threefold-Work of the Holy Spirit* in the life of the believer.

The following is a brief definition of how each term is used in this study:

○   The **INDWELLING**, is the work of the Holy Spirit, given to every believer, which gives us everything we need to have, and to experience, the fullness of a personal relationship with God.

○   The **FILLING**, is the work of the Holy Spirit, available to every believer, to give us what we need, so we can have effective personal relationships with other people.

○ The **EMPOWERING**, is the work of the Holy Spirit, available to every believer, which gives us that special *power* we need for effective spiritual service.

The Indwelling for Our Relationship With God

Let us start by looking at the *Indwelling of the Holy Spirit*. This is the first area of the Holy Spirit's *Three-fold Work* in the life of the believer. The *Indwelling is the work of the Holy Spirit, which gives us **everything we need for a personal relationship with God**.*

If you were stranded alone on a desert island, and never saw another person in your life, with the *Indwelling of the Holy Spirit*, you would have all you need to enjoy, and to maintain the fullness of your *personal relationship with God*. That is very important to understand.

The Holy Spirit is the Third Person of the Trinity. When you are born again, He comes and lives in you. You do not receive part of Him, you receive all of Him. The Holy Spirit is not some liquid, like gasoline, He is a person. You do not drive up to God and say, give me half a tank of Holy Spirit. *Either you have all of Him or you do not have Him at all.*

I will never forget the time in my life when I misunderstood this. I was looking for more of the Holy Spirit, so I could have a more dynamic personal relationship with God. As I stood in my living room, looking out the window at the beautiful fall colors, this wonderful feeling flooded my soul. It was as though God Himself was speaking to me. I did not hear any audible words but I could feel them inside of me. They said, *What are you looking for? You already have the Holy Spirit. You have all of me you need. All I want is more of you.* What a peace I experienced. I did not receive any more of the Holy Spirit that day; I already had all of Him. On that day, I just came to accept that clear teaching of Scripture. The Holy Spirit is a Pwerson and I have all of Him. What a joy! I understood I truly had the Holy Spirit. Since that day, I have never questioned the fact I have the Holy Spirit living in me.

All believers receive the *Indwelling of the Holy Spirit* when they are saved (1 Corinthians 6:19-20; John 14:16-18; Romans 8:9; Galatians 4:4-7).

> But ye are not in the flesh, but in the Spirit, if so be that the Spirit of God dwell in you. Now if any man have not the Spirit of Christ, he is none of His.
>
> Romans 8:9

The *Indwelling of the Holy Spirit* is part of what makes New Testament believers the children of God.

> But as many as received Him, to them gave He power to become the sons of God, even to them that believe on His name.　　　　John 1:12

The Scriptures clearly teach, Old Testament believers were saved but did not have the *Indwelling of the Holy Spirit*. This was because Jesus had not yet died for their sins and been glorified. Having the *Indwelling of the Holy Spirit* is one of the most wonderful things about living in New Testament times. Prior to the cross, believers only had the Holy Spirit *with them*, to help them (John 14:17). Sometimes He came *upon them*, to fill them with *power* for a certain task, but He did not permanently *indwell* them.

Since the death, burial and resurrection of Christ, all believers have the Holy Spirit living *in* them (John 7:38-39; 14:17; Hebrews 11:39; 1 John 4:4).

> He that believeth on me, as the scripture hath said, out of his belly shall flow rivers of living water. (But this spake He of the Holy Spirit, which they that believe on Him should receive: for the Holy Ghost was not yet given; because that Jesus was not yet glorified).
>
> John 7:38-39

> And I will pray the Father, and He shall give you another Comforter, that He may abide with you forever; even the Spirit of Truth; whom the world cannot receive, because it seeth Him not, neither knoweth Him: but ye know Him; for He dwelleth **with you**, and shall be **in you**.
>
> John 14:16-17

The *Indwelling of the Holy Spirit* is the first part of the *Three-fold Work of the Holy Spirit* in the life of the Believer. Because of the *Indwelling*, we receive many benefits. The following are some things the Holy Spirit does for the believer, as part of the *Indwelling*:

He Seals

The Holy Spirit seals all those who are *Indwelled* by the Holy Spirit.

> Who hath also sealed us, and given us the earnest of the
> Spirit in our hearts.   2 Corinthians 1:22

The word *seal* is the translation of the Greek word, **sphagizo**. It means *to stamp with a signet*. A signet is a stamp or ring with initials, or a symbol, to identify an individual. In Bible times, people used a signet, in place of a signature, to affix their mark on things. The seal identified ownership. It also indicated the owner's approval of a transaction. Kings and heads of state have used signets and seals for thousands of years.

One time, when I was in a marketplace in Korea, I had an artist do a drawing for me. When he finished the drawing, he took out a small block of wood, with Korean letters on it, placed it on an inkpad and stamped the corner of the drawing. I asked him what the resulting mark was. He explained it was his signet. He said he stamped the work to identify it as his.

The Holy Spirit applies God's signet to us. He seals us, identifying us as belonging to God. This takes place immediately when we place our faith in Christ for salvation.

> In whom ye also trusted, after that ye heard the word of
> truth, the gospel of your salvation: in whom also after
> that ye believed, ye were sealed with the Holy Spirit of
> promise.   Ephesians 1:13

The sealing not only identifies us as His, but also keeps us until we stand before God in Heaven.

> And grieve not the Holy Spirit of God, whereby ye are
> sealed unto the day of redemption.
>   Ephesians 4:30

He Sanctifies

The Holy Spirit also sanctifies believers as part of the *Indwelling*. *Sanctify*, is not a uniquely religious word. To sanctify means to *set apart something for a specific purpose*. The concept of setting things aside for a unique purpose is not uncommon.

As I was growing up, we had some funnels in our house, which were set apart *(sanctified)* for specific purposes. Even though the funnels were identical, their usage was unique. One funnel was set apart for the kitchen. We used it to pour liquids, like cooking oil, from one container to another. In the garage, we had another funnel. That funnel was also used for pouring liquids through, like transmission fluid, coolant or motor oil.

One day, I needed to put oil in my car. That car was one of those models where you had to reach down and around something to get the oil in. That was back in the days when oil was in a can without a spout. In order to reach that difficult spot without spilling the oil all over the place, I needed a funnel. I could not find the funnel in the garage, so I went into the house and looked for something to use. I found something in the kitchen I was sure would work. It was a funnel, just like the one I used in the garage. That funnel was used to pour cooking oil through. It would certainly handle motor oil. When I was done, I went back to the kitchen, washed the funnel and put it back where it belonged. Everything looked fine.

Shortly after that incident, I was to learn the importance of sanctification *(setting something apart for a specific purpose)*. A few days after putting oil in my car, with the kitchen funnel, I decided to make some French Fries. I poured some peanut oil into a pot and fried some French Fries. They tasted good. When I was done, and the oil cooled down, I took the kitchen funnel and poured the oil back into the container, so it could be used again.

A few days later, I had a desire to have some of those delicious French Fries again. I poured some peanut oil into the pot, heated it up and cooked some French Fries. This time, for some reason, they did not taste the same. They picked up an unusual taste. My brother said they tasted like motor oil.

Even though I washed out the funnel, when I used it for motor oil, the oil penetrated the pores in the funnel. When I poured the cooking oil back into the container, through that funnel, the motor oil joined the other oil. That kitchen funnel could no longer be used in the kitchen. From that incident, I learned the importance of setting things apart for a specific use.

God wants to sanctify us *(set us aside for a specific purpose)* as believers. He does not want the old oil of the world to be placed in vessels He has set apart. He wants them to contain the fresh oil of the Holy Spirit. That is called *sanctification*.

Some Evangelicals differ as to the nature and extent of Biblical sanctification. Some believe sanctification is instantaneous, some believe it is a process. In a sense, they are both right.

There are Three Stages to Our Sanctification:

1. **Sanctification is the Work of the Holy Spirit Where He *Sets Us Apart Unto God*, the Moment We Place Our Faith in Him** (Romans 15:16; 1 Corinthians 1:2; 6:11; Acts 26:18).

> And such were some of you: but ye are washed, but ye **are sanctified**, but ye are justified in the name of the Lord Jesus, and by the Spirit of our God.
> 1 Corinthians 6:11

That part of sanctification is beyond our control. It is something God does the moment we are saved. This part of our sanctification is complete. This is where God says, *you are mine.* He distinguishes us from the rest of the world.

Even though we are all people, those people who believe in the Lord Jesus Christ are set apart by God, for Him, just like the funnels being designated kitchen funnels or garage funnels. The funnels were made by the same manufacturer, and very virtually identical, but they were set apart for a different place and function.

2. **Sanctification is Also the Daily Process Where the Holy Spirit** *Continues to Set Us Apart From Sin and Unto God* (1 Thessalonians 4:3; 5:23; 1 Peter 3:15; 2 Corinthians 3:18).

> For this is the will of God, even your sanctification, that ye should abstain from fornication.
> 1 Thessalonians 4:3

> But sanctify the Lord God in your hearts...
> 1 Peter 3:15

This part of sanctification is a daily process, which requires our cooperation. It is also like the funnels. Both funnels could be used in the kitchen or in the garage. Personally, I do not use kitchen funnels in the garage anymore, they give food a bad taste. In the same way, God does not want us to allow ourselves to be used for sin. It gives us a bad taste. We must determine to remain set apart for God. To do this, we need the Holy Spirit's help every day.

3. **Sanctification is Also Our Trust and Hope as We Look to the Future Return of Christ. At That Time, Our Bodies Will Be Changed. We Will Be Separated From Our Former Sinfulness, and From This Sinful World. We Will Have a New Body and a New Home. We Will Be Forever Separated From Sin** (Romans 8:15-23).

> And not only they, but ourselves also, which have the firstfruits of the Spirit, even we ourselves groan within ourselves, waiting for the adoption, to wit, the redemption of the body.
> Romans 8:23

Some groups use the term *Entire Sanctification*, to refer to a state of *sinless perfection*. They believe all believers; through the Holy Spirit can attain *sinless perfection*, while they are still living in this present world. They believe the Holy Spirit can bring us to a place where we do not sin anymore. Holiness groups hold to that position. I believe it stems from a misunderstanding of the *Three-fold Work of the Holy Spirit* and the *Three Stages of Sanctification*.

I know, as long as I live in this sinful body on this sinful world, I will never achieve *sinless perfection*. The Apostle Paul never got to that place either. He explained his daily struggle with sin in Romans 7:1-25.

> For I know that in me (that is, in my flesh,) dwelleth no good thing: for to will is present with me; but how to perform that which is good I find not. For the good that I would I do not: but the evil which I would not, that I do.
> Romans 7:18-19

In a *practical way*, it is true believers, with the help of the Holy Spirit, do not *have* to sin (1 John 2:1). We can call on God and claim His *power* to avoid sin. However, we do not arrive at the point *positionally* (the place where we will not sin), until after we are resurrected and have a new body. It is then, and only then, we will experience sinless perfection (1 Corinthians 15:42-54).

> For this corruptible must put on incorruption, and this mortal must put on immortality.   1 Corinthians 15:53

He Teaches

One special benefit we have, because of the *Indwelling of the Holy Spirit*, is His teaching ministry.

Man cannot *fully* grasp spiritual truths. We are finite beings and have a hard time understanding infinite concepts.

Have you ever tried to understand the future? Imagine all that lies ahead, countless years filled with countless possibilities. All of eternity lies ahead of us. That is overwhelming.

What about the past? Have you ever tried to comprehend the idea there is an eternal past? Everything on earth had a beginning, but what was there before that? Some scientists tell us we came from a big bang, but even that teaching raises the question, where did that big bang come from? There is an eternity past. God and His explanation of it all, laid out in the Bible, are the only logical explanation. Yet man has a hard time grasping that. Though there is enough evidence to point to the

Biblical model for God, creation and our existence, it takes the Holy Spirit's help for us to accept it fully and to comprehend it.

> Which things also we speak, not in the words which man's wisdom teacheth, but which the Holy Ghost teacheth; comparing spiritual things with spiritual. But the natural man receiveth not the things of the Spirit of God: for they are foolishness unto him: neither can he know them, because they are spiritually discerned.
> 1 Corinthians 2:13-14

It is the Holy Spirit who enables us to comprehend spiritual truths (John 14:26; 1 Corinthians 2:6-16).

> But the Comforter, which is the Holy Ghost, whom the Father will send in my name, He shall teach you all things, and bring all things to your remembrance, whatsoever I have said unto you.   John 14:26

We have the responsibility to study the Word of God and to ask the Holy Spirit to teach us. He can make the truths from the Word of God come alive in us. Just as He did when He gave me the very real assurance, I had the Holy Spirit. That truth was based in Scripture; it was not some new revelation. The Holy Spirit made it come alive.

Sometimes it takes much Bible study over an extended period, before the Holy Spirit will confirm a truth to you. Whether He confirms it to you or not, if it is in the Word of God, it is still the truth.

The Holy Spirit also uses *Pastors* and *Teachers* to help instruct us. When they minister in the *power* of the Spirit, He is actually the one teaching us (Ephesians 4:11-16; 2 Timothy 2:2).

He Leads & Guides

Another special benefit of the *Indwelling of the Holy Spirit* is we can have His leading and guiding. It is a real joy to know God wants to lead us.

Over the years, I meet many believers who have never known the joy of having God lead them. The reason they do not have God leading them is simple. It is because they do not *allow*

Him to lead them. They live like unbelievers. Instead of reading or listening to God's Word and following His clear teaching, they wait for God to convict them of wrong or questionable practices in their lives. Often they will say something like this; *I'll change when the Lord convicts me.*

The word *convict (reprove)* means *to identify as guilty.* God intended the convicting work of the Holy Spirit for the unsaved (John 16:8-11). Unlike the unsaved, the Holy Spirit does not have to **convict** the believer, because He can **lead** us into all truth (John 16:13). It is a lot nicer to be led than to be convicted.

> And when He is come, He will reprove *[convict]* the world of sin, and of righteousness, and of judgment.
> John 16:8

> Howbeit when He, the Spirit of Truth, is come, He will guide you into all the truth...　　　　John 16:13a

This is not a benefit for an elite few. The leading and guiding of the Holy Spirit is available to all believers. God wants to walk with us and direct our paths on a daily basis. He does this through the Holy Spirit.

We do not have to stumble through life, or wander aimlessly. We can know God's will for our life each day. All we need to do is pray; listen to His Word, and allow the Holy Spirit to lead us. Then, as James H. Sammis, put it so well, in his hymn, we can, *Trust and Obey, for there's no other way, to be happy in Jesus, but to trust and obey.*

> For as many as are led by the Spirit of God, they are the sons of God.　　　　Romans 8:14

He Assures

The *Indwelling of the Holy Spirit* gives the believer assurance of salvation. We can know for sure we are saved. Not only does the Bible tell us so, but also the Holy Spirit assures us.

> The Spirit itself beareth witness with our spirit, that we are the children of God.　　　　Romans 8:16

> These things have I written unto you that believe on the
> name of the Son of God; that ye may know that ye have
> eternal life, and that ye may believe on the name of the
> Son of God.   1 John 5:13

It is wonderful to know we truly are saved. We can base our assurance of salvation on the written Word of God, yet we also have the added dimension of the assurance of our salvation from the Holy Spirit.

I have met too many believers who are tormented, not having assurance of their salvation. They need to stop listening to men, or to their own doubting hearts, and start listening to the Word of God and to the Holy Spirit. When they do, they will find freedom from fear and doubt.

He Intercedes

The Holy Spirit has an interceding ministry, which He does on behalf of all believers, as part of the *Indwelling*. This is one of the hardest for me to understand. I find it totally amazing to know God still loves me, and provides an Intercessor for me, even though I still sin and fail Him.

Sin is awful. No one makes us sin. When we sin, it is something we *choose* to do. That sin separates man and God (Isaiah 59:2). As a believer, when I sin, in God's amazing grace, I can confess that sin to Him (1 John 1:9). He then lets the Holy Spirit come and intercede on my behalf. That is possible because of the finished work of Christ on the cross. Christ is our Mediator. He died to make a way for us to be accepted by God (1 Timothy 2:5; Hebrews 8:6).

> For there is one God, and one mediator between God and
> man, the man Christ Jesus.   1 Timothy 2:5

The Holy Spirit is our Intercessor. Because of what Christ provided for us, by securing our salvation, the Holy Spirit can serve as our Intercessor bringing our requests and needs to the Father.

> Likewise the Spirit also helpeth our infirmities: for we
> know not what we should pray for as we ought: but the

> Spirit itself maketh intercession for us with groanings which cannot be uttered. And He that searcheth the hearts knoweth what is the mind of the Spirit, because He maketh intercession for the saints according to the will of God.   Romans 8:26-27

The Holy Spirit does this intercessory work on behalf of all believers. We do not need another person or priest to come before God on our behalf. We have direct access through the Holy Spirit.

When we have sinned or failed God, or when we find it hard to express our needs to God, the Holy Spirit intercedes for us. Many times, when we cannot find the right words to say, when all words seem like groans and muttering, the Holy Spirit takes our hearts concerns, puts them into the right words, and brings them before God on our behalf.

We have the confidence of answered prayer because the Holy Spirit, our Intercessor, brings our prayers before God.

He Comforts

Another wonderful benefit of the *Indwelling of the Holy Spirit* is His comforting ministry. Everyone knows what it feels like to be hurt. Sometimes uncaring people cause the hurt. Sometimes we cause the hurt by our own words or actions. Sometimes circumstances, beyond our control, seem to rush in and sweep away all our joy and hope. Many times, we face those pains alone.

Though sometimes people may surround us, many times they never know the hurts we are experiencing; sometimes they do not even care. It is an awful feeling of desperation when life's difficulties press on you and you feel all alone (Proverbs 14:10).

It is an awful feeling to hurt and not have anyone there to care or to help comfort you. What a joy and comfort it is to know God cares. There have been a number of times in my life when only the comfort of the Holy Spirit saw me through the dark days.

As part of the *Indwelling*, the Holy Spirit is available to be the *Counselor* and *Comforter* for all believers (John 14:16, 26).

> And I pray the Father, and He shall give you another Comforter, that he may abide with you for ever.
>
> John 14:16

This is one of the dearest ministries of the Holy Spirit. There will be sometimes when the Holy Spirit will be our only Comforter. It is a wonderful blessing to know, all we need to do is call on Him and He will always be there for us.

He Provides

The Lord's provision is another great benefit of the *Indwelling of the Holy Spirit*. It is amazing to realize Jesus made everything we will ever need available to us and that He uses the Holy Spirit to provide those needs (Ephesians 1:3; Philippians 4:19).

> Blessed be the God and Father of our Lord Jesus Christ, who hath blessed us with all spiritual blessings in heavenly places in Christ.　　Ephesians 1:3

> But my God shall supply all your need according to His riches in glory by Christ Jesus.　　Philippians 4:19

The Holy Spirit is the instrument through whom God works to meet the needs in our lives. Though God expects us to work, to help provide the needs for our families, the Holy Spirit gives us the ability to do the work we do.

When we do our part, there will be times God will intervene in unexplainable ways to provide for us.

> For I know that this shall turn to my salvation through your prayer, and the supply of the Spirit of Jesus Christ.
>
> Philippians 1:19

Whatever we need, God will provide for us, through His Holy Spirit. He will provide not only our spiritual needs, but also our physical and emotional needs. All we need to do is to call on Him (Matthew 7:7-8).

He Gives Gifts

One of the other benefits of the *Indwelling of the Holy Spirit* is the *Spiritual Gift* God brings to life in us. Everyone has a *Spiritual Gift* (1 Corinthians 12:1-6; Romans 12:4-8). That *gift* is given new life as part of the *Indwelling of the Holy Spirit*.

> Now there are diversities of gifts, but the same Spirit.
> 1 Corinthians 12:4

Our *Spiritual Gift* helps make us unique as individuals. Each *Gift* comes with its own *perspective* on life and gives us a unique *potential* for service. Our *gift* focuses on *who we are*, rather than on *what we do*.

To utilize our *Gift*, effectively, we need the *Filling* and *Empowering* of the Holy Spirit. We will look at the *Gifts* in more detail in another chapter.

Some people are content to stop with just the *Indwelling of the Holy Spirit* and never know the joy of using their *gift* because they never seek to be *filled* or *empowered* by the Spirit of God. They have a personal relationship with God, but they do not know the *fullness of the Holy Spirit* in their relationships with others or in service.

Conclusion

The Holy Spirit has a *Three-fold Work* He wants to undertake in the life of every believer. The first work is the *Indwelling*. Every born again child of God, has the *Indwelling of the Holy Spirit*. We do not need another work of the Holy Spirit to bring us any closer to God. We must realize this truth and accept it. The other two works of the Holy Spirit have a different purpose. To be all God wants us to be, and to know *fullness* of joy in your Christian life, you need the other two works of the Holy Spirit.

In the next chapter, we will look at the second aspect of the *Three-fold Work of the Holy Spirit*. We will see what it means to be *Filled with the Holy Spirit*.

CHAPTER EIGHT

QUESTIONS

Verse to Memorize: Romans 8:9

8.1   Why is it important to understand what people mean by the words they use to describe the work of the Holy Spirit?

8.2   Give a brief definition of the *Indwelling*, the *Filling* and the *Empowering* of the Holy Spirit.

8.3   Who is *Indwelled* by the Holy Spirit and when does it occur?

8.4   What is the difference between how the Holy Spirit *Indwells* the New Testament believers and how He worked in the lives of his people in the Old Testament?

8.5   What are some of the benefits of having the *Indwelling of the Holy Spirit*?

QUESTIONS FOR ADDITIONAL THOUGHT

8.6   Discuss the concept that the *Indwelling* of the Holy Spirit is all one needs for a personal relationship with the Lord. Why might someone be satisfied with just the *Indwelling*? What is the danger of that?

8.7   What are some of the problems, which arise when someone thinks a believer does not have the *Indwelling* of the Holy Spirit until some point after they are saved?

8.8   What does the Bible say regarding the teaching of Entire Sanctification?

CHAPTER NINE

The Holy Spirit and The Saved: The Filling & The Fruit

The Filling
For Relationships with People

The *Filling* of the Holy Spirit is the second area of the *Three-fold Work of the Holy Spirit*, in the life of the believer. **This is the work of the Holy Spirit whereby we allow Him to fill and control each area of our lives, so we can have effective relationships with others, and thus reflect the Lord Jesus Christ in our lives.**

The *Filling* is not for our personal relationship with God, we received all we needed for that when we were *Indwelled by the Holy Spirit*. Upon salvation, you received all of the Holy Spirit. You have either all of Him or none of Him. The *Filling* focuses on how much of *You* He has.

If you were alone on a desert island, you would not need the *Filling of the Holy Spirit*. However, if you are around people, the *Filling of the Holy Spirit* is **absolutely necessary**. We need it to enable us to deal effectively with people the way God wants.

God is concerned about how we get along with others. How can we let others know of His wonderful love and grace, if we do not get along with people? He knows it is very important, so He gave us the Holy Spirit to help us in this area.

Many Christians have a *Cultural Christianity*. What that means is, even if they were not saved, they would still do many things in their life the same way, especially in their relationships with others. They would still be kind. They would still be honest in their business dealings. They would still avoid immorality. That sounds good but it is not. What they are really saying, though they may not realize it, is they could still do all those things without the Holy Spirit. It also means they are probably doing all those things right now, without asking the Holy Spirit for help. That means many Christians are living most of their lives in the power of the flesh.

Abraham Lincoln, a godly man and one of America's greatest presidents, understood the need for God's help in every area of his daily life. He acknowledged that need by his daily prayers. An incident in his life also reflected His understanding of this important principle. One day, he was walking down the street with another man. They came upon a drunk in the gutter. Abraham Lincoln stopped to help the man. Lincoln's companion was taken back. Lincoln said to him, *There, but for the grace of God, go I.* Lincoln knew his own goodness was not enough. He understood the need to depend on God for daily living.

If you do not ask God to control or enable you in your daily living, especially in your relationships with others, then you are doing it in your own strength. Though you may not realize it, that means you are living in your own strength. That means little, of eternal significance, is happening in your life. God wants us to realize we need His help, especially for daily living and our relationships with others. He wants to give us His strength. He knows the flesh will fail us, but His strength will never fail.

The Filling Explained
Ephesians 5:18-21

And be not drunk with wine, wherein is excess; but be filled with the Spirit; speaking to yourselves in psalms and hymns and spiritual songs, singing and making melody in your heart to the Lord; giving thanks always for all things unto God and the Father in the name of our Lord Jesus Christ; submitting yourselves one to another in the fear of God.

Ephesians 5:18-21

Being *Filled with the Holy Spirit* is not an option for the believer. In Ephesians 5:18, God commands us to be *Filled with the Holy Spirit.* To understand this command properly, you must view it in its context. Verse 18, is part of one sentence. The sentence starts in verse 18, and runs through verse 21. The key words are, *be filled* (controlled), and *submitting yourselves.* We have the *Filling of the Spirit* when we submit ourselves to the

Holy Spirit for His *power* to help us with our daily relationships with others.

You must recognize you do not need more of the Holy Spirit, but He needs more of you. If you will acknowledge your need for His help and *yield control* of your life to Him, He will *fill* you.

Some prefer a more dynamic interpretation of the *Filling*. They would rather have it be a dramatic *super spiritual* experience, with some type of outward, elaborate results, rather than accepting the fact the *Filling of the Spirit* comes from the discipline of *yielding* yourself to the Lord for strength to handle your daily relationships. The *Filling of the Spirit* is a miraculous working of God, but it is often bestowed quietly in a non-flamboyant way *upon* those who seek it.

Though it may not seem miraculous to some, we need the *Filling of the Spirit* if we are to relate effectively to other people the way God wants.

Ephesians 5:18, compares the effects of the *Filling* to the effects of drunkenness. When a person is drunk, they are subject to an *external control* and experience an *outward personality change*. To have effective relationships with others, we need to submit ourselves to the Holy Spirit so He can fill us and control each area of our lives. He will do this in such a way others see a change in us which reflects Christ.

There are many **Personal Benefits**, when we are *Filled with the Spirit:*

○ It helps us in our relationships with others, which makes our life a lot better.

○ It keeps us in prayer and constant dependence on God throughout the day.

○ It puts Scripture and a song on our lips (v.19).

○ It puts a melody in our hearts (v.19).

○ It enables us to see God working in all situations (v.20).

To be *Filled with the Holy Spirit*, you must submit to God and yield your rights to Him in your relationships with others (v.21). I find it helpful to do this, in the form of a prayer of commitment, at the beginning of each day. Then, throughout the day, as I deal with various people, I pray silently to be *filled* again and again. God answers those prayers.

The Filling and Our Daily Relationships
Ephesians 4:1-5:17; 5:22-6:9

> I therefore the prisoner of the Lord, beseech you that ye walk worthy...   Ephesians 4:1

If you read Ephesians 4:1-6:9, you will see the *Filling of the Holy Spirit* is dealt with in the context of the life of the believer and our daily living relationships. The Bible is so practical. Ephesians shows us specific ways the believer should live in relationship to others.

Too often, we live each day relating to others in our own strength. Many believers do not realize they need the *Filling of the Holy Spirit* to have effective daily relationships with others. It is impossible to do what these verses say without the *Filling of the Holy Spirit*.

Without the *Filling of the Holy Spirit*, our relationships are conducted in the flesh. No matter how sincere your love for God, unless you ask and allow the Holy Spirit to *fill* you for your daily relationships, you are doing it your own strength. When we realize that and allow the Holy Spirit to *fill* us, it will transform every area of our lives.

The passage of Scripture, which commands us to be *Filled with the Spirit*, addresses **Four Types of Relationships where we need the Filling of the Holy Spirit**:

O   **Church-Body Relationships** (4:1-16).
     Relating to Other Christians.

     We need the *Filling of the Holy Spirit* to have effective relationships with other believers. You cannot consistently do what these verses call for, without the Holy Spirit.

...walk worthy of the vocation wherewith ye are called, with all lowliness, and meekness, with longsuffering, forbearing one another in love.

Ephesians 4:1-2

...till we all come in the unity of faith...

Ephesians 4:13

...speaking the truth in love...

Ephesians 4:14

...the whole body fitly joined together and compacted by that which every joint supplieth, according to the effectual working in the measure of every part, maketh the increase of the body unto the edifying of itself in love.

Ephesians 4:16

It would make a tremendous difference in our churches, if believers would ask the Holy Spirit to *fill* them as they relate to other Christians. We do too many of our relationships in our own power. That is why we have so many conflicts in our churches. If we would allow the Holy Spirit to *fill* (control) us each time we relate with other believers, we would see His love and His *power*, and experience the unity He wants us to have.

O   **Non-Church Relationships** (4:17-5:17).
Relating with Those Outside of the Church.

We need the *Filling of the Holy Spirit* to have effective relationships with those outside of church.

How can we be the light of the world (Matthew 5:14) if we do not specifically seek to allow the Holy Spirit to shine His light through us? The reason so many of our daily encounters with unbelievers are so unfruitful is too often we fail to ask the Holy Spirit to *fill* us. We need to be *Filled with the Holy Spirit* to effectively relate to the unsaved people we encounter in our daily lives. Everyone needs to see Jesus. They will not see Jesus in us, nor can we do anything these verses say we should do, unless we are *Filled with the Holy Spirit*.

...walk not as other Gentiles walk...

Ephesians 4:17

...put off concerning the former conversation...

Ephesians 4:22

...put on the new man...   Ephesians 4:24

...putting away lying, speak every man truth with his neighbour...   Ephesians 4:25

...be ye kind one to another, tenderhearted, forgiving one another...   Ephesians 4:32

...but walk in love...   Ephesians 5:2

...have no fellowship with the unfruitful works of darkness...   Ephesians 5:11

..walk circumspectly, not as fools, but as wise..

Ephesians 5:15

It would make a tremendous difference in our towns, in our neighborhoods, and in our countries, if believers would ask the Holy Spirit to *fill* them as they relate to the unchurched, wherever they are. What a transformation would occur. It would not be long before many of the unchurched became believers.

○ **Family Relationships** (5:22-6:4).
Relating to Relatives.

We need the *Filling of the Holy Spirit* to have effective relationships in our homes and with our relatives.

Few people ask the Holy Spirit to *fill* them in their homes for their daily relationships with their families. Most people try to relate to their families in their own strength. Too often, it seems we only seek the Holy Spirit's help in our families when trials and conflicts arise. Joy and peace would fill our lives if we would realize we need the *Filling of the Holy Spirit* every day to do what these verses say.

Wives, submit yourselves unto your own husbands...

Ephesians 5:22

Husbands, love your wives...   Ephesians 5:25

Children, obey your parents...   Ephesians 6:1

Fathers, provoke not your children to wrath...

Ephesians 6:2

It would make a wonderful difference in our homes, if believers would ask the Holy Spirit to *fill* them every day, and throughout the day, as they relate to their family members. Our homes would become more like Heaven on earth.

O   **Occupational Relationships** (6:5-9).
Relating to those we work with or for.

We need the *Filling of the Holy Spirit* to have effective relationships in our work place, with those we work *with* and those we work *for*.

Too often, we view our work as secular and think God is not interested in secular things. We usually do our jobs, relating to those in the workplace, in our own strength. We must realize our job is a spiritual matter. God gives it to us to give us a platform to show Him to others. We must have the *Filling of the Holy Spirit* to be able to relate to others in the work place the way God wants us to relate to them.

Servants *[employees]*, be obedient to them that are your masters *[employers]*...   Ephesians 6:5

...Masters *[employers]*, do the same things unto them *[employees]*...   Ephesians 6:9

What a difference it would make in the places where we do business, if believers would ask the Holy Spirit to fill them as they relate to others in their business dealings. God would be glorified and many more businesses would be blessed.

The necessity of the *Filling of the Holy Spirit* is dealt with in the book of Ephesians, right in the middle of this teaching on relationships. That shows us we need to be *Filled with the Holy Spirit* for our relationships with other people. If properly understood, this one teaching on the Holy Spirit could transform your life and the world around you. Imagine how different this world would be if all believers understood and applied this truth to their lives. In this world of darkness, we would be like a city set on a hill, whose light would shine for all the world to see.

> Ye are the light of the world. A city that is set on an hill cannot be hid.   Matthew 5:14

The Filling and Our Walk

In Scripture, the *Filling of the Holy Spirit* is also called, *our walk*. As we are *Filled with the Holy Spirit*, He enables us to walk, living as God would have us to live, around and with other people.

The *Filling* does not focus on our relationship with God, or our service for Him, though we must have a right relationship with God to be *filled* and we must be *filled* to serve Him. **The *Filling* focuses on what we allow the Holy Spirit to do in and through us, each day of our lives.** It implies action on our part.

Every day, when I ask the Holy Spirit to *fill* me, I am acknowledging I need Him. I yield control to Him and He responds by helping me walk *(live)*, the way He wants me to live.

Notice how the word *walk,* appears numerous times in the context on the *Filling of the Holy Spirit*:

> I therefore, the prisoner of the Lord, beseech you that ye **walk** worthy of the vocation wherewith ye are called.
>   Ephesians 4:1

> This I say therefore, and testify in the Lord, that ye henceforth **walk** not as other Gentiles **walk**, in the vanity of their mind.   Ephesians 4:17

> And **walk** in love...   Ephesians 5:2a

> For ye were sometimes darkness, but now are ye light in the Lord: **walk** as children of light.
>   Ephesians 5:8

> See then that ye **walk** circumspectly, not as fools, but as wise.   Ephesians 5:15

One sure sign you are *Filled with the Holy Spirit*, is when you seek to allow God to do, in and through you, what He wants to do, not just on Sunday but every day of the week.

The Filling and the Fruit of the Spirit

The *Fruit of the Holy Spirit* is directly related to the *Filling*. Too many believers look for the Fruit as something inwardly provided by the Holy Spirit, for their own benefit. That is a misunderstanding. A tree produces fruit for others, not itself. The Holy Spirit produces the *Fruit of the Holy Spirit* in our lives, for others, as we are *Filled with the Holy Spirit*.

The *Fruit of the Spirit* in your life *evidences* the *Filling of the Holy Spirit* to others.

> But the Fruit of the Spirit is love, joy, peace, longsuffering, gentleness, goodness, faith, meekness, temperance: against such there is no law.
>
> Galatians 5:22-23

> For the fruit of the Spirit is in all goodness and righteousness and truth.   Ephesians 5:9

The Fruit of the Spirit, is that which the Holy Spirit produces in us, as we *walk (are filled by Him)*. This fruit can be clearly seen and enjoyed by those around us, in the same way trees produce their fruit for others.

In the context of Galatians 5:1-6:10, where it speaks of the *Fruit of the Holy Spirit*, it clearly focuses on our relationships with others:

> ...but by love serve **one another**.   Galatians 5:13

> For all the law is fulfilled in one word, even in this; Thou shalt love **thy neighbor** as thyself.
>
> Galatians 5:14

> If we live in the Spirit, let us also walk in the Spirit. Let us not be desirous of vainglory, provoking **one another**, envying **one another**.   Galatians 5:25-26

> Bear ye **one another's** burdens, and so fulfill the law of Christ.   Galatians 6:2

135

> As we have therefore opportunity, let us do good to **all
> men**, especially unto them which are of the household of
> faith.   Galatians 6:10

Notice the word *walk* (5:25), a synonym for the *Filling*, is used in this context. It is our *walk*, as we are *Filled with the Spirit*, which enables us to relate effectively to those around us, the way Christ would have relate.

As we allow the Holy Spirit to *Fill* us *(as we walk in the Spirit)*, He produces *Fruit* in our lives (5:22-25). He gives us love, joy, peace, longsuffering, gentleness, goodness, faith, meekness and temperance. These become evident to others. This *Fruit* is not for us, it is for us to share with others.

The **Fruit of the Spirit** is different from the **Fruit of a Christian** (John 15:1-8).

> Herein is my Father glorified, that ye bear much fruit; so
> shall ye be my disciples.   John 15:8

The **Fruit of a Christian** is reaching other people for the Lord, so they can in turn reach others for the Lord. That comes, as you are *Filled with the Spirit* and especially when you have the *Empowering for Service*.

Conclusion

What a joy it is when believers, who already have the *Indwelling of the Holy Spirit*, allow God to *Fill (control)* them.

This *Filling* adds a special dimension to each of our relationships and makes all of them take on eternal significance. If more believers would understand and apply this truth, it would transform our homes, our churches and even our world.

In the next chapter, we will look at how we need to take the next step and allow God to *Empower* us with the Holy Spirit for service.

CHAPTER NINE
QUESTIONS

Verse to Memorize: Ephesians 5:18

9.1   What is the purpose of the *Filling of the Holy Spirit*?

9.2   How is the *Filling* similar to being drunk?

9:3   What are some of the personal benefits of being *Filled with the Holy Spirit*, which help us in our relationships with others?

9:4   What are some of the relationships, outlined in Ephesians, for which we need the *Filling of the Holy Spirit*?

9:5   How does the word *Walk,* relate to the *Filling*?

9:6   How does the *Fruit of the Spirit* differ from the *Fruit of a Christian*?

QUESTIONS FOR ADDITIONAL THOUGHT

9.7   Why does God have to command us to be *Filled with the Holy Spirit*?

9.8   Identify how the *Filling of the Holy Spirit* can make a difference in your personal relationships as you seek to serve Him. Use comparison and contrast techniques to illustrate your points.

Dr. Larry A. Maxwell

CHAPTER TEN

The Holy Spirit and The Saved: The Empowering for Service

What is the Empowering for Service?

The *Empowering* of the Holy Spirit is the third distinct area of the *Three-fold Work* of the Holy Spirit's ministry, in the life of a believer. *This is the work of the Holy Spirit, where He sovereignly comes upon believers to empower them for a specific ministry.*

This is not for the believer's personal relationship with God (2 Corinthians 1:21-22) nor is it for their relationship with others, though one should be *Indwelled* by, and *Filled with the Holy Spirit*, to experience the real *fullness* of His *power* for service.

This *Empowering* is temporary in most cases, though it does not have to be. From what we see in the Bible, **God gives us the Empowering to help us accomplish a specific task or ministry at a particular point in time.** This is something we must remember to request from God each time we seek to serve Him.

This aspect of the Work of the Holy Spirit most closely parallels the work of the Holy Spirit in the lives of God's people in the Old Testament. This is where He comes *upon* someone to *empower* him or her for a specific task.

Different Names for the Same Thing

Various people, and even Scripture itself, sometimes use different names for the *Empowering*. That can cause confusion if someone does not look carefully at the context. Sometimes the term *Filling* (which also describes a completely different work of the Holy Spirit), is used to describe the *Empowering*.

In the Bible, when the term *Filling*, is used to describe the *Empowering*, it refers to being *filled* with the *power* of the Holy Spirit, rather than to being *Indwelled by the Holy Spirit* or *controlled* by the Holy Spirit for daily relationships. This *filling*, which refers to the *Empowering*, can be, and often is, much more dynamic than the *Filling of the Holy Spirit* for daily relationships.

Great men of God recognized the need for this and spoke about the necessity of a work of the Holy Spirit to *empower* them for service. Evangelist John R. Rice called it the, *Baptism of the Spirit*. When he spoke in soul-winning conferences around the world, he challenged others to yield themselves to God, so the Holy Spirit could give them soul-winning *power*.

Many Pentecostals & Charismatics refer to the *Baptism of the Holy Spirit* as a special work of the Holy Spirit, which believers must seek, and which takes place after salvation. Some of them confuse it with the *Indwelling of the Holy Spirit*, and view it as something, which gives you more of the Holy Spirit for a closer personal relationship with God. Some of them confuse it with the *Filling of the Holy Spirit*, and view it as something, which helps them in their relationships with others.

Some people, especially non-Charismatics, use the term, *Baptism of the Holy Spirit*, to refer to the *Indwelling of the Holy Spirit*. This is based primarily on two verses: John 1:33 and 1 Corinthians 12:13.

Let us look at what John the Baptist said in John 1:33:

> And I knew Him not: but He that sent me to baptize with water, the same said unto me, Upon whom thou shalt see the Spirit descending, and remaining on Him, the same is He which baptizeth with the Holy Ghost.
>
> John 1:33

In each of the Gospel accounts, there is a reference to this statement by John the Baptist, that Christ would baptize with the Holy Ghost (Matthew 3:11; Mark 1:8; Luke 3:16 and John 1:33). The accounts rendered in the Gospels of Matthew and Luke, say, *baptizeth with the Holy Ghost **and** with fire.*

In Acts 1:5, before Jesus ascended into heaven, He told the disciples they would *be baptized with the Holy Ghost, not many days hence.* What did He mean by that?

Jesus did not mean the *Baptism* and the *Indwelling of the*

Holy Spirit were the same thing. The disciples already *received* the Holy Spirit prior to that. It occurred after Jesus rose from the dead, ascended to the Father and then appeared to them (John 20:21-22).

> Then said Jesus to them again, Peace be unto you: as my Father hath sent me, even so send I you. And when He had said this, He breathed on them, and said unto them, receive ye the Holy Ghost.
>
> John 20:21-22

In that first upper room, post-resurrection, pre-final ascension encounter with Christ, the disciples *received* the permanent *Indwelling of the Holy Spirit*. They were not able to *receive* the Holy Spirit prior to that because Jesus had not been glorified until that specific time (John 7:39). When Mary encountered the risen Christ at the tomb on Easter morning, she did not *receive* the Holy Spirit because, though Christ had risen, He had not ascended to the Father and not been glorified at that time (John 20:17).

In the John 20:21-22 encounter, Christ returned to earth, after ascending to the Father. By that time, He was glorified, so His followers could, and did, receive the *Indwelling of the Holy Spirit*, as do all believers from that point forward.

Some try to teach the Holy Spirit came in a *transitional way* during the Book of Acts, starting on the Day of Pentecost. Neither Jesus, nor the Bible, said anything about the Holy Spirit coming transitionally. There was no need for Him to come transitionally. The only thing Jesus said, which prevented believers from being *Indwelled by the Holy Spirit*, was the need for Him to be glorified. Once He was glorified, all believers could receive the *Indwelling of the Holy Spirit*. The transitional teaching is a result of not distinguishing the *Indwelling of the Holy Spirit* from the *Empowering of the Holy Spirit*.

There is a big difference between what happened in John 20:21-22, and the Baptism of the Holy Spirit, which happened in Acts, on the Day of Pentecost. In John 20:21-22, the Holy Spirit came and *indwelled* the believers. There were not any outward manifestations or resulting action on their part.

However, in Acts, when they were *Baptized with the Holy Spirit*, He came *upon them* and *filled them with power*.

> By ye shall receive power, after that the Holy Ghost is come **upon you**...   Acts 1:8

> ...And there appeared unto them cloven tongues like as of fire, it sat **upon** each of them. And they were **filled** with the Holy Ghost...   Acts 2:3-4

Those passages do not say they were *Indwelled by the Holy Spirit*, nor that they *received* the Holy Spirit. What happened was clearly the Holy Spirit came **upon** them to **fill them with power for service**. That is the *Empowering of the Holy Spirit*.

This Baptism *(Empowering)* of the Holy Ghost occurred again at other times in the book of Acts. In Acts 11:15-17, Paul commented on one of those instances as he stood before the leadership of the church in Jerusalem. He commented about how some of the Gentiles at Caesarea, shared the same experience the disciples had on the day of Pentecost.

Paul said *the Holy Ghost fell on them, as on us... (v.15)*. Notice he used one of the words for the *Empowering*, the word *on*. The Gentile believers experienced the *Empowering of the Holy Spirit*, just like the Disciples.

The *Empowering* is not always as dramatic as it was on the Day of Pentecost, but it is as powerful.

Those who dispute this teaching and still claim the baptism John spoke of refers to the *Indwelling* of the Holy Spirit, use, 1 Corinthians 12:13, as a proof text for their teaching.

> For by *[en]* one Spirit are we all baptized into one body, whether we be Jews or Gentiles, whether we be bond or free; and have been all made to drink into one Spirit.
> 1 Corinthians 12:13

Notice how this verse links the baptism it speaks of, with being part of a church. Many Pentecostals and Charismatics, plus a number of Non-Pentecostal, Evangelical Bible scholars have been taught that verse speaks of God uniting believers in a Universal, Invisible Church, through the Holy Spirit. That is one commonly held interpretation. If it is correct, then this baptism is definitely not the same as what happened on the day of Pentecost, because what they received, as we have seen in the previous verses, was clearly the *Empowering of the Holy Spirit*, not the *Indwelling of the Holy Spirit.*

It is the *Indwelling of the Holy Spirit* which makes us part of the Family of God *(the universal body of believers they refer to).* If the baptism spoken of in 1 Corinthians 12:13, does make us part of the Family of God, it would have to be different from the baptism which John spoke of, and which was fulfilled on the Day of Pentecost. Perhaps, this could be one of the *baptisms* spoken of in Hebrews 6:1-2.

> Therefore leaving the principles of the doctrine of Christ, let us go on unto perfection; not laying again the foundation of repentance from dead works, and of faith toward God, of the doctrine of **baptisms**...
>
> Hebrews 6:1-2

There are a number of other scholars who believe 1 Corinthians 12:13, refers to Water Baptism, and that it is used to unite believers with a Local Church. They point out the original Greek word *en* translated as *by* in that passage, should be translated as *in*, making the passage read, *for in one spirit.*

No matter which position you take, regarding 1 Corinthians 12:13, it must be understood what happens in that verse is not the same as what happened on the Day of Pentecost. On the Day of Pentecost, the Bible makes it clear the believers were already *Indwelled by the Holy Spirit*. On that day, the Holy Spirit came **upon** the believers and they were *Empowered with the Holy Spirit for service.*

Evangelist Dwight L. Moody said he saw the Lord's hand of blessing on his ministry increase dramatically after he received the *power* of the Holy Spirit. He was not referring to the *Indwelling*, or to the *Filling*. Moody knew he already had the Indwelling *of the Holy Spirit*. He was referring to the *Empowering of the Holy Spirit.*

R.A. Torrey, another old-time evangelist, challenged people to seek the *Empowering of the Holy Spirit* for spiritual service. Torrey worked with Moody. Torrey knew every believer was

Indwelled by the Holy Spirit, but he knew they also needed a special measure of the Holy Spirit's *power* for service.

The Empowering Explained

One of the words used in the Scriptures for the *Empowering of the Holy Spirit*, is the *anointing* (**chrisma**). To understand the *Empowering of the Spirit*, it is necessary to look at what the Scriptures say about *anointing*.

In the Old Testament, the Priests were anointed.

> Then shalt thou take the anointing oil, and pour it upon his head, and anoint him.   Exodus 29:7

Oil, a symbol of the Holy Spirit, was placed on the head of the priests to set them apart for service. This symbolically showed the necessity of the Holy Spirit for service.

Kings were also anointed in the Old Testament.

> Then Samuel took the horn of oil, and anointed him in the midst of his brethren: and the Spirit of the LORD came upon David from that day forward.
> 1 Samuel 16:13a

Oil, the symbol of the Holy Spirit, was used when kings were anointed. The anointing conferred *power* and authority on the individual and reminded them of the need for the Holy Spirit's *power*.

The Old Testament anointing with *power* was something, which could depart. King Saul was anointed but then lost the *power* of God (1 Samuel 16:14).

> But the Spirit of the LORD departed from Saul...
> 1 Samuel 16:14

David had the anointing and prayed he would not lose the *Empowering* of God in his life (Psalm 51:11).

> Cast me not away from Thy presence; and take not Thy Holy Spirit from me.   Psalm 51:11

As an Old Testament believer, David did not have the *Indwelling of the Holy Spirit*, nor the *Filling of the Holy Spirit* for daily relationships with others. David did have the *Empowering of the Holy Spirit for service.* It was this *Empowering of the Holy Spirit* David did not want taken away.

In the New Testament, Jesus was called the **Christos** *(Greek)*, the Christ, which means the *Anointed* One (Matthew 1:1).

> How God anointed Jesus of Nazareth with the Holy Ghost and with power.   Acts 10:38a

In an earlier chapter in this book, we saw it was through the *Empowering of the Holy Spirit* Jesus ministered while here on earth.

On the Day of Pentecost, the Believers were *Empowered by the Holy Spirit.* They already *received* the *Indwelling of the Holy Spirit* from Christ, after the resurrection and glorification of Christ, and before Pentecost.

> Then said Jesus to them again, Peace be unto you: as my Father hath sent me, even so send I you. And when He had said this, He breathed on them, and saith unto them, Receive ye the Holy Ghost.
>
> John 20:21-22

Right before Jesus ascended into heaven, He told the disciples they would receive *power* for service later, when the Holy Spirit would come **upon** *them*, (the Old Testament terminology for the *Empowering of the Holy Spirit).*

> But ye shall receive power, after that the Holy Ghost is come **upon** you: and ye shall be witnesses unto me both in Jerusalem, and in all Judea, and in Samaria, and unto the uttermost part of the earth.   Acts 2:8

Notice the fulfillment of that promise, for the *Empowering of the Holy Spirit,* in Acts 2:1-4 (*upon* and *filled*), also the explanation in Acts 2:33 (*the promise of the Holy Ghost*) of what took place.

> And when the day of Pentecost was fully come, they were all with one accord in one place. And suddenly there came a sound from heaven as of a rushing mighty wind, and it filled all the house where they were sitting.

> And there appeared unto them cloven tongues like as of fire, and it sat **upon** each of them. And they were all filled with the Holy Ghost, and began to speak with other tongues, as the Spirit gave them utterance.
>
> Acts 2:1-4

> Therefore being by the right hand of God exalted, and having received of the Father **the promise** of the Holy Ghost, He hath shed forth this, which ye now see and hear.
> Acts 2:33

Later, in the Book of Acts, Paul met a group of believers in Ephesus, who never heard of the Holy Spirit (Acts 19:1-7). This classic example shows it is possible to be saved but not know about the Holy Spirit. The *Indwelling of the Holy Spirit* is not dependent on our knowledge of Him nor on our obedience to Him. It is given to us because of the completed work of Christ and His glorification.

The believers in this context had not even been baptized properly but had the *Indwelling of the Holy Spirit.* They did not have the *Empowering of the Holy Spirit.* When properly instructed, they were baptized and were then *Empowered with the Holy Spirit* for service, just as the disciples had been.

It is God's will for all believers to have the *Empowering of the Holy Spirit.* He wants us to be *anointed* with His *power.* Those who are anointed are, *anointed ones.* That is what the word *Christian* means.

> Yet if any man suffer as a Christian [*anointed one*], let him not be ashamed; but let him glorify God on this behalf.
> 1 Peter 4:16

Though every Christian can have the *Empowering* for Service, many do not. Perhaps it is because many do not serve the Lord, or perhaps it is because many want God's power for personal edification, which is not God's purpose. On the other hand, perhaps, it is because they do not know what the *Empowering* is and that it is something they need to seek.

God will sovereignly give us His *Empowering,* when we persistently ask Him for it, for His glory, so we can minister effectively to others. We must ask and serve, then ask and serve, and ask and serve. We must be as concerned and persistent about asking for the *Empowering of the Holy Spirit*, as a friend is who needs bread for a visitor, and who faithfully goes in search of bread and will not give up until he finds some. That friend is not seeking the bread for himself, but for the benefit of others.

> And He said unto them, Which of you shall have a friend, and shall go unto him at midnight, and say unto him, Friend, lend me three loaves; for a friend of mine in his journey is come to me, and I have nothing to set before him? And he from within shall answer and say, Trouble me not: for the door is now shut, and my children are with me in bed; I cannot rise and give thee. I say unto you, Though he will not rise and give him, because he is his friend, yet because of his importunity he will rise and give him as many as he needeth. And I say unto you, Ask, and it shall be given you; seek, and ye shall find; knock, and it shall be opened unto you.
>
> Luke 11:5-9

> If ye then, being evil, know how to give good gifts unto your children: how much more shall your Heavenly Father give the Holy Spirit to them that ask Him?
>
> Luke 11:13

We need to seek the *power* of the Holy Spirit, like the friend, who sought the bread, so we can get the *power* of the Holy Spirit to give the bread of life effectively to others.

The Empowering Illustrated

Various passages of Scripture show the *Empowering* of the Holy Spirit at work in the lives of God's people. The Bible makes a distinction made between having the Holy Spirit and having His *power*.

The prophet Isaiah, in the Old Testament, said he served the Lord in God's *power*.

> The Spirit of the LORD is **upon** me; because the LORD hath **anointed** me to preach...   Isaiah 61:1

The Apostle Paul said he ministered in the *power* of the Holy Spirit.

> And my speech and my preaching was not with enticing words of man's wisdom, but in demonstration of the **Spirit** and of **power**.
>
> 1 Corinthians 2:4

Paul called it *the power of His might*, (Ephesians 6:10). He said it is essential to have that *power*, as we enter any spiritual battle for the Lord.

> Finally, my brethren, be strong in the Lord *[salvation]*, and in the power of His might *[empowering]*.
>
> Ephesians 6:10

In Philippians 3:10, Paul said one of his desires was, *that I may know Him, and the power of His resurrection.* He served so many years in the *power* of the Lord, through the enabling of the Holy Spirit, yet after all those years he knew he still needed the *Empowering of the Holy Spirit*. If Paul continually sought the *Empowering* as he served Christ, so should we.

> That I may know Him, and the power of His resurrection, and the fellowship of His sufferings, being made conformable unto His death.
>
> Philippians 3:10

A Warning

There is a danger among those who have been saved for a while. They know they have the Holy Spirit but sometimes forget to seek God's *power*. They learn how to do things for the Lord and do them automatically, often without seeking God's *power*. They accomplish their job, and see some results from their ministry, because God blesses the ministry of His Word (Isaiah 55:11), but they do not see the *fullness* of blessing God wants them to have, because they have not asked Him for the *power of the Holy Spirit*. Though they may not realize it, they are sincere but are *sincerely wrong*. They are actually serving the Lord in their own strength and that will be frustrating and will fail.

> For the weapons of our warfare are not carnal, but mighty through God to the pulling down of strong holds.
>
> 2 Corinthians 10:4

The lack of God's *power* is one reason why many people get tired and discouraged serving the Lord. To see the *results* God wants us to have, as we minister for Him, we must seek God's *power* and minister in that *power*, not in our own *power*.

There are many times I catch myself serving God in my own strength. It is so easy to forget to ask the Lord to fill me with Holy Spirit *power*. We must constantly stay in the presence of God and ask Him to fill us with His *power* to serve Him. Then He can sovereignly come *upon* us in *power* and work in our lives to produce the magnificent *results* He wants to produce.

Conclusion

The *Empowering of the Holy Spirit* is necessary as believers seek to use their *Spiritual Gift* in service for the Lord. If more believers would be *Filled with the Spirit* for their relationships with one another, and then seek God's *power* to minister for Him, it would transform many lives and churches.

In the next chapter, we will take a brief look at how it is possible to sin against the Holy Spirit and hinder the work of the *Indwelling*, the *Filling* and the *Empowering of the Holy Spirit*.

CHAPTER TEN
QUESTIONS

Verse to Memorize: Acts 1:8

10.1   What is the *Empowering of the Holy Spirit*?

10.2   What was the significance of the oil used in the Old Testament anointing of the priests and kings?

10.3   How do we know it is God's will for all Believers to be *Empowered by the Holy Spirit*?

10.4   Who are some people in the Bible who said they knew they needed the *Empowering*?

10.5   Why does God bless the ministry of some people who are not *Empowered*?

QUESTIONS FOR ADDITIONAL THOUGHT

10.6   What is the significance of the term *upon*, in relationship to the teaching on the *Empowering of the Holy Spirit*?

10.7   What is a very real danger, in relation to the *Empowering of the Holy Spirit*, for people who have been saved for a number of years? Can you illustrate this with your life and ministry?

CHAPTER ELEVEN

Sins Against The Holy Spirit

What Are Sins Against the Holy Spirit?

Some of the most common sins people commit are sins against the Holy Spirit. Many people do not realize we can, and often do, sin against the Holy Spirit. The Bible teaches sinning against the Holy Spirit is a very serious offense. Sins against the Holy Spirit attack the very *power* of God in our lives. We must recognize what the sins against the Holy Spirit are, so we can avoid them. If you discover you have committed one of these sins, I urge you to deal with it right away.

The Bible clearly identifies **Three Specific Sins Against the Holy Spirit.** Each of these sins against the Holy Spirit attack one of His three major works in the life of the believer.

○ **Blaspheming the Holy Spirit**

○ **Grieving the Holy Spirit**

○ **Quenching the Holy Spirit**

These sins seriously affect us and those around us. **Blaspheming** the Holy Spirit prevents the *Indwelling*, **Grieving** the Holy Spirit stops the *Filling* and **Quenching** the Holy Spirit stops the *Empowering*.

Blaspheming the Holy Spirit

> Wherefore I say unto you, all manner of sin and blasphemy shall be forgiven unto men: but blasphemy against the Holy Ghost, it shall not be forgiven him, neither in this world, neither in the world to come.
>
> Matthew 12:31

The Bible says in Matthew 12:31, someone who *Blasphemes the Holy Spirit* will not be forgiven. That is a very serious statement. That makes it very important to understand what blaspheming the Holy Spirit means.

When most people hear the word *blasphemy*, they usually think of a serious spiritual offense. The word, *blasphemy* was not originally used in a religious context. It was a common word used to express an action people sometimes took against another person.

The word *blasphemy* comes from a combination of two Greek words: **blapto** (harm, injurious), and **phemi** (speak). It means *injurious speech*. It was used originally in reference to speaking badly of someone, of slandering a person or insulting someone with untrue remarks.

Blasphemy does not indicate idle talk. When the Bible uses the word *Blasphemy*, it means the person knows the full implications of what they are saying. A person who *blasphemes* God is very serious about what they are doing. They mean what they say.

People have always *blasphemed* each other. As people lost the fear of God and started to slander God more and more, the word took on a religious significance. During the First Century A.D., *Blaspheming God* became a legal offense, which called for the death penalty.

The Bible very clearly teaches, a person who *Blasphemes* Jesus can be forgiven. This is seen in the case of the thief on the cross. Two thieves were crucified with Jesus (Matthew 27:38-44). The plural word, *thieves,* is used in verse Matthew 27:44. That makes it clear, *both* thieves *Blasphemed Christ.*

> The thieves also, which were crucified with Him, cast the
> same in His teeth.   Matthew 27:44

Though both thieves *Blasphemed Christ,* one of the thieves repented and was forgiven (Luke 23:39-43).

> And he said unto Jesus, Lord, remember me when thou
> comest into thy kingdom. And Jesus said unto him,
> Verily I say unto thee, To day shalt thou be with me in
> paradise.   Luke 23:42-43

Those who *Blaspheme Christ*, or *Blaspheme God the Father*, may be forgiven, but Matthew 12:31, says a person who *Blasphemes the Holy Spirit* cannot be forgiven.

Some Bible scholars believe *Blaspheming the Holy Spirit* means to ascribe the work of the Holy Spirit in the life of Christ to Satan, and that such an act only could be done while Christ was personally living on earth. Hence, no one could be guilty of that today.

Some believe *Blaspheming the Holy Spirit* means to ascribe the work of the Holy Spirit to Satan. If that were true, then many *Non-Pentecostal, Non-Charismatics*, I have met, are guilty of this. I believe that sin falls under the category of *Grieving* or *Quenching the Holy Spirit*, rather than *Blaspheming* Him.

Another view, which I, and other Bible scholars, hold to, says *Blaspheming the Holy Spirit* is when a person who has clearly seen, and understood, the *power* of God, vehemently rejects it, thus rejecting faith in Christ and salvation. According to this view, such a person has hardened himself or herself and therefore cannot, and will not, receive Christ as their Savior.

A person who is born again, but is concerned if perhaps they *Blasphemed the Holy Spirit*, does not need to worry. Such concern is evidence one does not have a hard heart.

> The sacrifices of God are a broken spirit: a broken and a contrite heart, O God, thou wilt not despise.
>
> Psalm 51:17

Blaspheming the Holy Spirit is a sin, which only an unsaved person can commit. This sin stops an unsaved person from ever getting saved. It prevents them from being *Indwelled with the Holy Spirit*. That is not something a Christian can do.

Grieving the Holy Spirit

> And grieve not the Holy Spirit of God, whereby ye are sealed unto the day of redemption.
>
> Ephesians 4:30

Grieving the Holy Spirit is a sin many believers commit. I believe it is one of the most common sins we are all too often guilty of committing.

Grieving the Holy Spirit stops one from experiencing *the Filling of the Holy Spirit,* which is primarily to help our relationships with others. In Ephesians 4:30, the sin of *Grieving the Holy Spirit* is found in the context of a believer's relationship with others.

The word to *grieve,* **lupeo,** used in Ephesians 4:30, means *to inflict pain on someone* or *to cause someone sorrow.* It can mean either physical or emotional pain.

God is very concerned how we deal with other people.

> Then saith He unto the disciples, It is impossible but that offences will come: but woe unto him, through whom they come! It were better for him that a millstone were hanged about his neck, and he cast into the sea, than that he should offend one of these little ones.
>
> Luke 17:1-2

If we do not deal, with others, the way God wants us to, it not only hurts them, it hurts God, causes Him sorrow, and *Grieves the Holy Spirit.*

I believe *Grieving the Holy Spirit* is the most common sin people commit against the Holy Spirit. It is also the one most people do not deal with. There are many believers who have grieved the Holy Spirit by the way they treat others, either with their words or actions. Many people remain un-reconciled. It is sad many do not see the seriousness of this sin.

I have seen this sin tear homes and churches apart. Because of this sin, many believers never know the joy and *power* of the Holy Spirit.

Grieving the Holy Spirit will stop you from being *Filled with the Holy Spirit,* or it will cause you to lose the *Filling of the Spirit,* if you have it. Without the *Filling of the Spirit,* a person will lack the *power* of God.

Quenching the Holy Spirit

Quench not the Spirit.   1 Thessalonians 5:19

The third sin against the Holy Spirit is *Quenching* the Holy Spirit. This is another sin committed by many believers.

Quenching the Holy Spirit stops the *Empowering* of the Holy Spirit in a person's life.

The word for *quench*, **sbennumi**, used in 1 Thessalonians 5:19, means *to extinguish by drowning with water*. God is saying He does not want us to put out the fire of the Holy Spirit. That fire is the *Empowering* of the Holy Spirit for service.

Too often believers, by their words or actions, put out the fire of God's Spirit working in their own life, or in the lives of others. Because of that *Quenching*, they lose the *Empowering* of the Holy Spirit.

This has happened in my life many times. It seems there is always someone waiting to pour water on the fire of enthusiasm. I met some whom I believe do this unintentionally, but it is still *Quenching* the Holy Spirit. I have met others who seem to do delight extinguishing the fire of God. For some people, it seems *Quenching* the Holy Spirit is their way of life.

Many times, we *Quench* the Holy Spirit in our own lives when we do not love others as Christ loved us. We also *Quench* the Holy Spirit when we do not reach out to those God places in our lives, or when we do not minister our *gift*. In those cases, the sad thing is, we put out the fire of God in our own hearts.

We must be careful we do not *Quench* the work of God. Instead of *Quenching* the Holy Spirit, we should be *encouraging* the work of God. We need to fan the flames of the fire of God, not *Quench* them. If we want to *quench* something, we should work at *quenching* the fiery darts of the devil.

> Above all, taking the shield of faith, wherewith ye shall be able to quench all the fiery darts of the wicked.
>
> Ephesians 6:16

Dealing with These Sins

When we discover we have sinned against the Holy Spirit it is very important to deal with that sin right away. Unconfessed sin does not cause us to lose our salvation but it causes us to lose the *power* of the Holy Spirit and intimate fellowship with God.

Though you may unintentionally sin against the Holy Spirit, you are still accountable for it. Perhaps you did not realize what *Grieving* or *Quenching* the Holy Spirit was. If you discover you have done either of these, you must deal with them.

The Biblical way to deal with sin is to *confess it* and *forsake it* (1 John 1:9).

> If we confess our sins, He is faithful and just to forgive us our sins, and to cleanse us from all unrighteousness.
>
> 1 John 1:9

The word *confess* is the Greek word, **homologomen**, it means *to agree with, to think the same about something*. To confess your sin means *you must agree with God you have sinned and think the same way about that sin as He does*. God hates all sin and wants it out of our lives.

If your sin against the Holy Spirit involves other people, such as offending others or pouring out their fire for God, not only must you confess it to God, you must also go to those people and seek to be reconciled to them (Matthew 5:23-24).

> Therefore if thou bring thy gift to the altar, and there rememberest that thy brother hath ought against thee: Leave there thy gift before the altar, and go thy way; first, be reconciled to thy brother, and then come and offer thy gift.
>
> Matthew 5:23-24

Unconfessed Sin and *Unreconciled Believers* are two serious problems, which plague the church. Too many believers sin against God and sin against each other and never deal with it. That is one of the reasons so many churches do not experience the true fullness of God. No amount of service, sacrifice or singing is sufficient to satisfy God's demands that we be reconciled to Him and to others.

If more believers would follow the Biblical admonitions for confession of sin and reconciliation, God could fill more of His people, and His church, with His wonderful *power*.

Conclusion

As we saw in this chapter, it is very common for people to sin against the Holy Spirit. The consequences of such sin are very serious. We must carefully guard our hearts so we do not allow any of those sins in our lives.

If we become aware we have committed any of the sins against the Holy Spirit, we must confess and forsake them.

If you discovered and dealt with any sins against the Holy Spirit in your life, you are ready to move on to the next chapter, where we will look at the area of the *Gifts of the Holy Spirit*. That area works in conjunction with the *Indwelling*, the *Filling* and the *Empowering* of the Holy Spirit.

CHAPTER ELEVEN
QUESTIONS

Verse to Memorize: 1 John 1:9

11.1 Why is it important to know what the sins against the Holy Spirit are?

11.2 What does it mean to Blaspheme the Holy Spirit?

11.3 What does it mean to Grieve the Holy Spirit?

11.4 What does it mean to Quench the Holy Spirit?

11.5 What should a person do if they become aware they have committed a sin against the Holy Spirit?

QUESTIONS FOR ADDITIONAL THOUGHT

11.6 How would you deal with someone who was afraid they Blasphemed the Holy Spirit?

11.7 How have you seen the sins against the Holy Spirit in action as you have served the Lord? How could such sins be avoided in the future?

CHAPTER TWELVE

The Gifts of the Holy Spirit
The Outline & Results

The Warning
1 Corinthians 12:1-3

Some of the greatest confusion and division among Christians today is regarding the *Gifts of the Holy Spirit*. Some very good people take very different stands on this topic. As you approach this topic, it is important to look carefully at the Scriptures and set aside any presuppositions you may have.

In Christian circles today, there seem to be two mutually exclusive and almost diametrically opposed positions on the *Gifts of the Holy Spirit*. People often identify where they stand on the *Gifts of the Holy Spirit* by classifying themselves as either *Pentecostal* and/or *Charismatic* or as *Non-Pentecostal and/or Non-Charismatic.*

Supporters of the *Pentecostal* or *Charismatic* positions, usually focus strongly on tongues, healing, miracles and prophesy. On the other side are their opponents, those who believe the teaching on tongues, healing, and miracles and prophesy, as set forth by those two movements, are not Biblical or are not for today.

One of the main problems, which causes a lot of the confusion and division, is too many people have accepted the modern day definitions, rather than the Biblical definitions, relating to the work of the Holy Spirit. This is especially true with the terms: tongues, healing, miracles and prophesy. What comes to you mind when you hear those words? If you approach any study with the wrong definitions, your study will be flawed.

In a later chapter in this book, we look at the historical background and specific beliefs associated with the *Pentecostal* and *Charismatic Movements.* You will see how, and why, they have had such a powerful influence on people's perception of the Holy Spirit.

While the *Pentecostals* and *Charismatics* enthusiastically promote their teachings, their opponents often conduct their approach in an adversarial manner and try to explain away those teachings.

To counter the *Pentecostal* and *Charismatic* teaching, the explanations used by many *Non-Pentecostal/Non-Charismatics*, often rely heavily on intricate, expanded definitions of Greek words and special uses of tenses in the original languages *(uses not agreed upon by many scholars, even within their own camp).*

I have seen too much misuse of the original languages. Some like to impress others and cause them to believe they alone have the proper interpretation because of their special knowledge, and their mastery of the original languages.

> ...Knowledge puffeth up, but charity edifieth.
>
> 1 Corinthians 8:1b

Careful exposition of the Scriptures is important. Proper study of the Biblical languages will only reinforce, or enhance, what is clearly taught in the reliable translations of the Scriptures, which we have in our own language. Some teaching relies primarily on complicated, controversial Biblical language exposition, and rules or shades of meaning, which are only accepted by scholars who hold to one particular school of thought. If that type of scholarship is the only way, to either support or disprove a position, then there is a good possibility something may be wrong with that exposition.

The Bible was not given to us as a Greek or Hebrew Grammar book. It seems too many scholars lose sight of that. Knowledge puffs some up to think only those, who can expound the original languages, are competent to explain the scriptures. Such reasoning intimidates others and is wrong (1 Corinthians 4:6; 8:1; Isaiah 47:10). When properly used, understanding of the original languages is helpful. It will serve to reinforce and enhance the clear teachings of Scripture. The problem is too often a person's supposed mastery of the original languages is misused.

One of the common teachings, among the *Non-Pentecostal/Non-Charismatic* teachers, is to use certain phrases and tenses in Greek to explain how tongues, healing, miracles and prophesy were transitional *gifts* and are no longer around. They teach those *gifts* were only given temporarily during a period extending from Pentecost to sometime shortly after the middle of the Book of Acts. They use verses like 1 Corinthians 13:8-13, to substantiate their position.

> Charity never faileth: but whether there be prophecies, they shall fail; whether there be tongues, they shall cease; whether there be knowledge, it shall vanish away. For we know in part, and we prophesy in part. But when that which is perfect is come, then that which is in part shall be done away.
>
> 1 Corinthians 13:8-10

They claim, *that which is perfect*, refers to the completed written New Testament. They claim tongues and prophesy were given temporarily to authenticate the Word of God and then were no longer needed. They also use unique Greek language rules, developed by some theologians, to reinforce their teaching. That teaching is flawed in that it accepts modern, rather than Biblical, definitions of terms and because it relies heavily on special controversial Greek interpretation.

That is actually a relatively new teaching to accommodate a *Non-Pentecostal* viewpoint. That teaching arose to explain away *Pentecostal* and *Charismatic* doctrines. In attempting to prove one's doctrinal prejudice, it blurs the clear distinction between the Old and New Testaments by inserting that transitional period. Such teaching clouds the significance of the finished work of Christ on the cross and the distinctive role the Holy Spirit has under the New Covenant *(Testament)*.

Those of the *Pentecostal* and *Charismatic* schools of thought rightly challenge that transitional interpretation. They also counter that reactionary interpretation, with Romans 11:29.

> For the gifts and calling of God are without repentance.
>
> Romans 11:29

It is not necessary to react to each other's teachings, nor is it necessary to accept the flawed modern definition of terms. Nor do we need to turn to hidden meanings, only found in controversial interpretation of the original languages, in order to explain the working of the Holy Spirit.

My belief, which I try to explain in the next few chapters, is that tongues, healing, miracles and prophesy, as well as other workings of the Holy Spirit, are still around today. However, I do not believe they are what many *Pentecostals* or *Charismatics* teach they are. Nor do I believe they are what many of their opponents think they are. I also dispute the notion of a transitional period. It was never foretold in the Old Testament, nor spoken of by Christ. The Scriptures are clear; there is an Old Testament and a New Testament, not an In Between Testament.

I believe the modern controversy surrounding the work of the Holy Spirit, clouds the original teaching, has divided God's people, and has robbed the church of the *power* God intends it to have. People on both sides of this controversy, are often sincere believers, but I believe many of them are *sincerely wrong.*

God knew this controversy would happen. That is why He gave us a warning in 1 Corinthians 12, as He began to address the subject of the *Gifts of the Holy Spirit.*

> Now concerning spiritual gifts *[pneumatikon]* brethren, I would not have you ignorant.
> 1 Corinthians 12:1

Notice the warning found in 1 Corinthians 12:1-3, at the beginning of the teaching on things pertaining to the *Gifts of the Spirit.* The Bible says we should not be *ignorant* regarding this teaching. God knows we will have a tendency to misunderstand this teaching and He warns us. He wants us to understand this area of the *Gifts of the Spirit* and wants us all to have the same interpretation.

It is important to understand the Biblical teaching regarding this area of *Spiritual Gifts.* When properly understood, it will unite instead of divide.

> Endeavouring to keep the unity of the Spirit in the bond of peace.
> Ephesians 4:3

Understanding this teaching will help a person see the unique way God designed each of us and will reinforce the need to interrelate with other believers through the Local Church, so we can effectively serve the Lord.

In 1 Corinthians, chapters 1-11, Paul dealt mainly with things in the physical realm, which were troubling the Corinthians, such as food and clothing. Then, in chapter 12, he turns to addressing *things of the spirit* (**pneumatikon**). He begins this teaching by saying it is important we do not misunderstand this important doctrine.

> Ye know that ye were Gentiles, carried away unto these dumb idols, even as ye were led.
>
> 1 Corinthians 12:2

In verse 2, He warns us to remember *who* we were and *where* we came from. He reminds the Corinthians they used to believe and do some foolish things. In their past, they were sincere and thought they were right and thought they were pleasing God, but they were wrong. God makes the point is it is possible to believe you are right on this issue, yet be wrong.

> Wherefore I give you to understand, that no man speaking by the Spirit of God calleth Jesus accursed, and that no man can say that Jesus is the Lord, but by the Holy Ghost.
>
> 1 Corinthians 12:3

In verse 3, He warns how some may go as far as to question another person's salvation because of their position on the *Gifts of the Spirit*. He reminds us the test of a person's salvation, and acceptance into fellowship, must be basic. If someone says *Jesus is accursed,* obviously they are not saved. On the other hand, if they can wholeheartedly say *Jesus is Lord*, they are believers.

In verse three, in the phrase, *no man **can** say,* the Greek word, **dunatai**, is translated as **can**. **Dunatai** means, no man *has the power* to say. That means they cannot say it on their own. In the same verse, the word **say** is the translation of the Greek word, **lalon**. **Lalon** means *to make a hearty spontaneous confession.* Those words reinforce the teaching, *no man has the power to make a hearty spontaneous confession that Jesus is Lord, but by the Holy Ghost.*

It is possible to disagree on this important doctrine, regarding the work of the Holy Spirit, and still be brothers and sisters in Christ. It would be better if we could come to the agreement God wants us to have on this doctrine. I believe common ground can be found in outline in the next verses, I first learned this from my professors, Larry Coy and Ed Hindson.

The Outline
1 Corinthians 12:4-6

Now there are diversities of **gifts**, but the same Spirit. And there are differences of **administrations**, but the same Lord. And there are diversities of **operations**, but it is the same God which worketh all in all.

1 Corinthians 12:4-6

After the warning, in verses 1-3, the passage goes on to give us an outline of the area of *Spiritual Gifts*. It identifies three distinct areas: *Gifts, Administrations* and *Operations*, each one related to a different member of the Trinity.

Sometimes people confuse the *Gifts, Administrations* and *Operations*, just as they confuse the different members of the Trinity with each other. For example, people pray to Jesus, yet the Bible clearly says we are to pray to our Heavenly Father (Matthew 6:9). Some people refer to Jesus living in their heart, yet the Bible says Christ dwells in our hearts through the Holy Spirit (Ephesians 3:16-17).

Each member of the Trinity is distinct, yet each is God. The same is true with the *Gifts, Administrations*, and *Operations*. They are all related to each other, but the Scripture says they are each different.

One of the greatest causes of confusion comes from people who take the different passages of Scripture, which list the *Gifts, Administrations* and *Operations*, and combine them into one master list and call them all *Spiritual Gifts*. Since some of the same words appear in the different lists, people eliminate what they view as duplicates. Following that method, and being influenced by their own view of the *Pentecostal* or *Charismatic* movements, different scholars arrive at different lists of *Gifts*. I have seen lists ranging from seven to twenty-one gifts.

There is a serious problem with that method of interpretation. God gave us a specific outline, clearly distinguishing between *Gifts, Administrations* and *Operations*. Each of these is clearly delineated in Scripture, without any partial or duplicate lists. God wants us to understand clearly these important truths. He is not the author of confusion (1 Corinthians 14:33).

If we follow the outline God gave us in 1 Corinthians 12:4-6, and identify the specific lists of *Gifts, Administrations*, and *Operations* found in Scripture, for what they really are, it will eliminate a lot of confusion.

The outline God gives here helps us see clearly, there is a difference between the *Gifts*, the *Administrations*, and the *Operations*.

1.   Gifts (Motivations)

> Now there are diversities of gifts, but the same Spirit.
> 1 Corinthians 12:4

The word *gifts,* is the translation of the Greek word, **charismaton.** It means *a favor bestowed that causes one to rejoice inwardly*. The emphasis is on inner joy. Our *spiritual gift* gives us inner joy, as we exercise it.

Everyone has a *Spiritual Gift*. Though there are certain things we do because of our specific *gift*, our *gift* focuses more on *what we are*, instead of on *what we do*. Our *spiritual gift* gives us a particular *perspective* on life and the *potential* for service. When we develop and exercise the abilities God has given us, it provides us with a certain outlook and joy. It gives us a particular inner *motivation*.

Though the *Gifts* are mentioned in this outline, they are not listed in 1 Corinthians. The Corinthians had a problem with the *Ministries* and *Results*, so Paul focused on those instead of on the specific *gifts*. The list of *Gifts* is found in Romans 12:3-8.

There are *Seven Different Gifts of the Spirit*. Everyone has one of the *Seven Gifts* (motivations). We are looking at the Outline now but will look at each of the *Gifts* in the next chapter.

> Having then gifts differing according to the grace that is given us, whether **prophesy**, let us prophesy according to the proportion of faith; or **ministry**, let us wait on our

ministering: or he that **teacheth**, on teaching; or he that **exhorteth**, on exhortation: he that **giveth**, let him do it with simplicity; he that **ruleth**, with diligence; he that **sheweth** mercy, with cheerfulness

Romans 12:6-8

Our **Gift** *(Motivation)* is **ACTIVATED** by the Holy Spirit.

2. Administrations (Ministries)

And there are differences of administrations, but the same Lord.   1 Corinthians 12:5

The word *administrations,* is the translation of the Greek word, ***diakonion***. It means *the service of a servant, an office or position, a ministry.*

This word *administrations* ***(diakonion)*** is used many times in the New Testament. It has various shades of meaning. The context determines its particular meaning. Here it refers to our *Ministry.*

Every believer should have a *Ministry.* Unlike our *Gift,* which focuses on what we *are*, our *Ministry* focuses on what we *do*.

There are a variety of *Ministries* listed in Scripture. Almost any *Spiritual Gift* can be used in any *Ministry*. People with different *Gifts* from each other can have the same *Ministry*.

Two Categories of Ministries are set forth in Scripture:

O   **Ministries *to* Various Churches.**

Five *Areas of Ministry* are given to minister *to* various churches. These are set forth in Ephesians 4:11-16.

And He gave some **apostles**; and some, **prophets**; and some, **evangelists**; and some **pastors** and **teachers**.   Ephesians 4:11

O   **Ministries which Minister Primarily *within* One Church.**

Eight *Areas of Ministry* are given for use *within* each Local Church. These are found in 1 Corinthians 12:28.

> And God hath set some in the church, first **apostles**, secondarily **prophets**, thirdly **teachers**, after that **miracles**, then **gifts of healings, helps, governments, diversities of tongues**.
>
> 1 Corinthians 12:28

We will look at these *Two Categories of Ministries,* in more detail, in a later chapter.

Our **Ministry** is **ASSIGNED** by Jesus, through the Holy Spirit.

3. Operations (Manifestations/Results)

> And there are diversities of operations, but it is the same God which worketh all in all.
>
> 1 Corinthians 12:6

The word *operations,* is the translation of the Greek word, ***energematon.*** It means, *an effect, a result.*

The Operations are the different *Results,* which God sovereignly gives, when we use our *Gift* in a *Ministry.* We have no control as to what results God will give. Usually God gives a variety of results, in different people we encounter, as we use our *gift* to serve Him.

Nine Results are set forth in, 1 Corinthians 12:7-10.

> But the manifestation of the Spirit is given to every man to profit withal. For to one is given by the Spirit the **word of wisdom**; to another the **word of knowledge** by the same Spirit; to another **faith** by the same Spirit; to another the **gifts of healing** by the same Spirit; to another the **working of miracles**; to another **prophesy**; to another **discerning of spirits**; to another **divers kinds of tongues**; to another **the interpretation of tongues**.
>
> 1 Corinthians 12:7-10

The results, listed in verses 7-10, are sovereignly given by God and vary from person to person.

> But all these worketh *[energei]* that one and the selfsame Spirit, dividing severally as He will.
>
> 1 Corinthians 12:11

We can know our *Gift* and we can know the *Ministry* where we use our *Gift*, but we will never know in advance, the *Results* God will choose to give, when we use our *gift* in a *Ministry* to serve Him. God will sovereignly give a variety of *Results*, which will bring glory to Him.

The **Results** are **ALLOWED** by the Father.

This outline, regarding the *Gifts, Administrations* (Ministries) and *Operations* (Manifestations/Results), is so important to understand. To disregard, or discount, this outline, which God clearly gave us, can lead to many mistakes in your interpretation.

God clearly sets forth a distinction between the *Gifts*, the *Administrations* (Ministries) and the *Manifestations* (Results). Each is distinct and has a specific part in God's plan. Our goal should be to identify and understand them.

The Manifestations - Results
1 Corinthians 12:7-11

Let us look closer at the *Manifestations of the Spirit*. The *Manifestations* are the *Results* God says He gives when we use our **Gift** in a **Ministry** for Him. Though a person may use their *gift* in one particular *Ministry*, it is important to understand the *Results* in the lives of those touched by that ministry will be different.

It is interesting to note that immediately after presenting the *Outline on Spiritual Gifts*, God turned immediately to the issue of the various *Manifestations* (Results), which occur when people use their *Spiritual Gift* in *Ministry*.

Many people in the Corinthian Church were caught up in external things. God never lists the *Gifts* for them. Instead, He focuses on what happens as a *Result* of the *Gifts*.

The *Manifestations* (Results), listed in 1 Corinthians 12:7-11, appear to be a complete list but it is possible it may only be a partial listing of some of the results. The *Results* will vary as the Holy Spirit determines the needs (v.7, 11). As we minister in the *power* of the Spirit, He can produce the *Results* which are

168

exactly what the people being ministered to need. These results come because of someone using their *Gift*, whether it is a *speaking gift* or not. When we do our part, it is not us but God, who sovereignly gives the results.

The following is the list of *Results* in this passage, which God says He gives in the lives of those we minister to. A possible explanation, based on the meaning of the word, and from forty years of observation in ministry is given for each.

1. Word of Wisdom

Wisdom *(sophia)* means having skillful insight. The Word of Wisdom, is where *God gives a person insight*, in response to your *ministry*. That insight gives them the understanding they need to deal with a particular area of life. It helps produce skillfulness in their life.

We all need wisdom to know how to apply God's truths to our lives. God can give a specific piece of wisdom to a person, by something you say or do, as you serve in the *God's power*.

2. Word of Knowledge

The Word of Knowledge *(gnosis)* is where *God gives a person some facts they need to know*.

There have been many times I needed a piece of information and received it through someone else ministering his or her *gift* for the Lord. That information literally transformed my life. It is like finding the last piece to a puzzle, or the missing ingredient in a recipe.

Sometimes what we need is just a little more information *(knowledge)*. God often sends someone to us with that information.

How do wisdom and knowledge differ from each other? Wisdom emphasizes *application*, knowledge emphasizes *information*.

3. Faith

Faith *(pistis)* is something we all need. When we minister in the *power* of the Holy Spirit, God can strengthen the Faith of others. Faith is one of the most crucial elements in life. We need faith for salvation (Ephesians 2:8-9). We also need faith to live a life pleasing to God (Habakkuk 2:4).

It seems every day our faith is bombarded (James 1:3). We all can use some more faith. We need the faith, which gives us the victory (1 John 5:4).

It is a real joy, to be used of God, to help strengthen another person's faith.

4.   Gifts of Healing

Gifts of Healing are another *Result* God can sovereignly give as someone uses their *Spiritual Gift* in a *Ministry* for Him.

Notice 1 Corinthians 12:9, does not say *gift* of healing (singular, as in a spiritual *gift*), but rather, *gifts* of healing (plural, as in birthday *gifts*).

God heals others, over and over again, when we minister for Him. We probably do not realize how often He does this, because much of the healing is on the inside, where we do not usually see the results at first.

God especially delights in making someone whole. He often does it from the inside out. Though God may choose to extend the inner healing outwardly to a physical healing, it is the inner healing which more people need. That inner healing can often result in physical healing. As it says in Proverbs 17:22, *A merry heart doeth good like a medicine.*

5.   Working of Miracles

One of the most outwardly exciting *Results* God gives, in response to someone using their *spiritual gift* in a *Ministry*, is the working of miracles. It is important to remember, this is not speaking of a *ministry* but of *results* God gives in other people's lives, in response to someone using a *spiritual gift* in *ministry*.

This *Result* is not to confirm a ministry, as Christ's miracles and the miracles of the Apostles did. This is something God gives for the primary purpose of benefiting the receiver (1 Corinthians 12:7). In this context, *Working of Miracles* is where God causes someone to have an outward working of the *power* of God in his or her life. God transforms people's lives, through His Spirit, in such a way others see the difference.

As you use your *gift*, in a *ministry*, with the *power* of the Holy Spirit, God can do wonderful, miraculous, life changing things in other people's lives, things, which can only be done by Him, in His *power*. Sometimes these workings are not explainable by the laws of nature. Those results are usually so obvious; other people can see them and glorify God for them.

6.   Prophesy

Prophesy is another *Result* God gives in response to someone using his or her *gift* to serve Him. The word prophesy, has various shades of meaning. Its primary meaning is *to proclaim the Word of God with authority*, so others understand what God wants them to know.

Sometimes prophesy means to *fore-tell* God's Word, that is, to proclaim events in advance. Quite often, it refers to *forth-telling* God's Word, which we usually call preaching.

Like all other words, the meaning of this word must be determined by its context. Prophesy, in this context is a result. It is where *God enforces a truth someone needs to know*. This is done in such a way the person can see something wrong in their life, which they need to correct, or something right, which they need to do (1 Corinthians 14:2). This results in helping to bring lives in line with the Word of God.

7.   Discerning of Spirits

Discerning of Spirits is another important result God gives in response to someone using their *gift* in *ministry*. This is where *God gives someone the perception to distinguish between truth and error* (Hebrews 5:14).

There is a lot of spiritual error in the world today. As you minister in the *power* of the Holy Spirit, God can use you to help others discern between truth and error.

Sometimes it is what you *do*, not what you *say* that helps people recognize the truth. Your living testimony, ministering your *gift* in your daily life, can help people see the validity of Christianity and the deceptiveness of cults and false teachers.

## 8.	Divers Kinds of Tongues

Remember this is a list of *Results* from someone else ministering. Divers Kinds of Tongues *(glossa)* is where *God enables someone to speak someone else's language*, in response to his or her *Ministry*. Perhaps this is mainly a *Result* of those whose *Ministry* is teaching others languages. Some people, are taught another language, but never can grasp the language. Others, with God's help, seem to pick up languages easily, when taught by the right person. *This could also refer to a supernatural enabling to learn another language.*

There is a tremendous need for the church to reach out beyond its own cultural confines and language groups and extend itself cross-culturally and multi-lingually.

In Matthew 28:19, God says we are to, *teach all nations.* The words *all nations*, does not mean *countries*, it means *people groups*. Nations are groups of people who have their own distinct culture. They often have their own language. Thousands of people groups, representing billions of people, do not speak your language. As you minister in the *power* of God, hopefully, some will get a burden to learn other people's languages so they can reach out to them in those languages, or help them learn their language. God can help them do it. Perhaps they will get the burden to get involved in the *Ministry of Linguistics*.

## 9.	Interpretation of Tongues

Interpretation *(hermeneia)* of Tongues is where G*od enables someone to clearly understand and explain someone else's language.* Not only must people learn to speak the language of other people, but also some must learn how to clearly interpret and expound in someone else's language.

As I traveled around the world and ministered to people in different language groups, I found there is clearly a difference between speaking a language and interpreting it. I have met some who can speak another language, other than their own, but who cannot interpret or expound it. I have also met some who can expound the Word of God, in a language which is not their own, but who cannot get up in front of people and speak it clearly. I have seen God enable people to do both, in response to someone else ministering in the *power* of the Holy Spirit.

Conclusion

The Outline God gives in 1 Corinthians 12:4-6, is one of the greatest tools in clarifying the teaching on the *Gifts of the Holy Spirit*.

We need to identify carefully the differences between the *Gifts, Administrations (Ministries)* and *Operations (Results)*. When we do that, God can give us the unity we need. We can then utilize our *Gift* in a *Ministry*. Then God can give the *Results*, which will bring honor and glory to Him.

In the next chapter, we will look at the specific listing of the *Gifts of the Holy Spirit*, which God gives us in Scripture.

CHAPTER TWELVE
QUESTIONS

Verses to Memorize: 1 Corinthians 12:4-6

12.1 What warning are we given in 1 Corinthians 12:1-3, regarding the teaching on this area of *Spiritual Gifts*?

12.2 What are the three areas, outlined in 1 Corinthians 12:4-6, regarding the teaching on *Spiritual Gifts*?

12.3 What do we mean by the term, *Gifts* of the Spirit?

12.4 What is meant by the term, *Administrations* of the Spirit?

12.5 What do we mean by, *Operations* of the Spirit?

12.6 What are some of the *Results* God gives, in the lives of others, as we use our *gift* in the *Power* of the Holy Spirit?

QUESTIONS FOR ADDITIONAL THOUGHT

12.7 Comment on the statement that much teaching regarding the *Gifts of the Holy Spirit* today is in *reaction* to the *Pentecostal* and *Charismatic Movements*.

12.8 Referring to the *Manifestations of the Spirit*, covered in this lesson, how have you seen these in response to your *ministry*?

CHAPTER THIRTEEN

The Gifts of the Holy Spirit
The Gifts

How Many Gifts Are There?

In this chapter, we are going to look at each of the *Spiritual Gifts*. As we saw in the last chapter, every person has a *Spiritual Gift*. Our *Spiritual Gift* gives us a particular *perspective* on life and the *potential* for spiritual service. It is that different perspective and potential, which distinguish the *Gifts* from each other.

Before we look at the individual *Gifts*, it is important to determine how many *Gifts* there are. It would seem there would be general agreement among Bible scholars on this matter. Yet, as I reviewed many books and listened to many sermons preached on this subject, I found very few agree as to how many *Spiritual Gifts* there are.

The problem, which prevents many from agreeing on how many *Gifts* there are, stems from the tendency to disregard the outline in 1 Corinthians 12:4-6. Perhaps, like me, most people never saw its significance. I believe many times the outline is discounted because of strongly held presuppositions and the danger it will jeopardize someone's system of belief.

It is important to understand God did not give us different lists of *Spiritual Gifts* in different places. Each list in Scripture, related to the topic of *Spiritual Gifts*, is something distinct and must be identified as such.

Those who disregard the *Outline on Spiritual Gifts*, usually blur the distinction between the *Gifts*, the *Administrations* (Ministries), and the *Operations* (Results). They include a mix of all of these, in their list of what they call *Spiritual Gifts*. This causes confusion. It is true, the *Ministries* and *Results* are linked with the *Gifts*, but they are distinctly different.

Besides blurring the distinctions God gave, those who combine the *Gifts, Ministries* and *Results*, and call them all *Gifts*, have another problem. They usually eliminate the words, which are repeated in the different lists of *Gifts, Ministries* and *Results*, seeing them as duplicates.

Some of the same words appear in the different lists because they refer to different things. For example, there is a *Gift of Teaching* and a *Ministry of Teaching*, both are distinct. There is also the *Spiritual Gift of Prophesy*, the *Ministry of Prophet* and *the Result of Prophesy*. Each one is different, as clearly seen in its respective context. The word *Apostle* is included in the list of *Ministries to the various Churches*, but it is also in the list of *Ministries within the Local Church* because they are different *Ministries*. None of these is a duplicate. In each case, the meaning is determined by the context. Those who combine the lists, and eliminate the repeated words, blur the distinctions God gives.

There is another problem among those who discount the *Outline on Spiritual Gifts*. From the final list they derive, many of the *Non-Charismatics* identify certain *Gifts* on their lists as no longer valid. They usually identify *Apostles, Prophets, Tongues, Miracles* and *Healing*, as *Sign Gifts*. They claim these were only *temporary gifts*. One problem with that is some of those never were *gifts*. This misunderstanding is usually due to accepting the wrong definitions of what those things are.

There are problems combining into one list, things God identifies as different. There is also a problem when we explain away something God has for today. Perhaps, unknowingly, the goal of justifying one's presuppositions causes otherwise excellent Bible scholars to err in this area. This is too important for us to allow so much confusion.

Accepting the outline from 1 Corinthians 12:4-6, and identifying the distinction between the *Gifts*, the *Ministries* and the *Results*, and properly defining what each one is, can eliminate a lot of confusion. It can also bring us the unity God intended us to have on this subject.

The only real differences we should have at all, on this subject, may be in relation to our extended definitions of what each *Gift, Ministry* or *Result* means.

The Gifts
Romans 12:1-8

There is only one place in the New Testament where it gives us a list of things it specifically says are the *Gifts*. That is Romans 12:6-8.

> Having then **gifts** differing according to the grace that is given us, whether **prophesy**, let us prophesy according to the proportion of faith; or **ministry**, let us wait on our ministering: or he that teacheth, on **teaching**; or he that exhorteth, on **exhortation**: he that giveth, let him do it with simplicity; he that ruleth, with diligence; he that sheweth **mercy**, with cheerfulness.
>
> Romans 12:6-8

Before the presentation of this list of the *Gifts of the Spirit*, God gives us some important introductory material, at the beginning of the chapter.

> I beseech you, therefore, brethren, by the mercies of God, that ye present your bodies a living sacrifice, holy, acceptable unto God, which is your reasonable service. And be not conformed to this world: but be ye transformed by the renewing of your mind, that ye may prove what is that good, and acceptable, and perfect, will of God. Romans 12:1-2

Verses 1-2, tell us we need to present our bodies to Christ, and allow Him to transform our minds, so we can know and experience the will of God in our lives. One of the reasons for our *Spiritual Gift* is to give us the *potential* for service. Dedication is always a pre-requisite for spiritual service. A proper dedication to God precedes a proper understanding of the *Gifts*.

> For I say, through the grace given unto me, to every man that is among you, not to think of himself more highly than he ought to think; but to think soberly, according as God hath dealt to every man the measure of faith.
>
> Romans 12:3

Verse 3 gives us a warning. We should not to think we are better than anyone else. No *Gift* makes anyone better than anyone else. That is very important to understand.

The *Gifts* enable us to relate together as a body, so we can effectively serve God and know the joy of doing His will on earth. Some *Gifts* give people a more *administrative perspective* on life, others a more *functional perspective*. Some *Gifts* focus on *speaking*, while others focus on *serving*.

Because of the importance of each *Gift's* unique *perspective*, when someone understands the importance of their *Gift*, there can be a tendency for one *Gift* to think it, or a few of the other *Gifts*, are more important than some others. We must watch out for that attitude. In this passage we are reminded, no *Gift* is any better than any other *Gift*.

> For as we have many members in one body, and all members have not the same office: so we, being many, are one body in Christ, and every one members one of another.   Romans 12:4-5

Verses 4-5, remind us, we are all part of a spiritual body, a Local Church. That body is made up of different parts. In some ways, it is similar to our physical bodies. Our physical bodies have a specific number of different parts, which depend on and interact with each other. That distinction, between parts and their interaction, help our body function smoothly and properly as a whole.

The same is true of the church. We are all different parts of a spiritual body. We are not all the same part. We need to accept our unique design and identity. Then we need to learn how to relate to the other parts in the body. Our *Spiritual Gift* is given to us to use in the context of the Local Church. We are part of that spiritual body and need the other members of the church to help us function together, to the glory of God.

It is interesting to note there are *Seven Gifts of the Spirit*. When all *Seven Gifts* are put together, and each do their part, the body can function as a whole and can fully manifest the work of the *Seven-fold Spirit* (Revelation 1:4; Isaiah 11:2), which causes God's Glory to be apparent (Ephesians 3:21).

How Many Gifts Do People Have?

I often hear people ask others the question, *How many Gifts do you have?* Though some people like to think they have many *Gifts*, the Scriptures teach us, each believer has only one *Gift*.

In the context of Romans 12:4-8, our *Gift* is referred to as a part of the body and each person is said to be **one** of those particular parts. That indicates each person only has **one** *Gift*.

Remember your *Gift* focuses on *who you are*. You cannot be an eye and an ear, nor a foot and a mouth, at the same time. However, you can be a foot in a mouth.

In 1 Peter 4:10, believers are exhorted to use *the gift*, they have been given by God.

> As every man hath received **the gift**, even so minister the same one to another...   1 Peter 4:10

Some people think they have more than one *Gift*. That may be because certain *Gifts* seem to function in a certain way, and appear to have areas where they overlap with other *Gifts*. In addition, various *Gifts* can be used in the same *Ministry*. Yet, it is important to remember, the scriptures are clear, each believer only has one *Gift*.

We are all only one part of the body. This should humble us and make us dependent on those with other *Gifts*, to compliment ours, so we can be effective in spiritual service.

Jesus was the only one who had all *Seven Gifts*.

> For in Him dwelleth all the fullness of the Godhead bodily.   Colossians 2:9

Our *Gift* gives us the *perspective* and *potential* to manifest one aspect of the fullness of Christ more naturally than the *Gift* other people have. When each of us allow God to manifest our *Gift* in us, together we can reflect God's glory as His church (Ephesians 3:20-21).

Some do not allow God to use their *Gift* in their lives. Perhaps that is why the Bible tells all of us to work at manifesting the characteristics of the other *Gifts*. Though that is not easy, we *need* to do that and *can* do it with God's help.

○ We are all told to give (Luke 6:38), which is the joy of the person with the **Gift of Giving**.

○ We are all told to keep our lives, and what we do, organized (1 Corinthians 14:40; Ephesians 5:15-17), which is the joy of the person with the **Gift of Ruling**.

○ We are all told to study (2 Timothy 2:15), which is the joy of the person with the **Gift of Teaching**.

○ We are all told to help others identify areas of change we and others need to make in our lives (Galatians 6:1), which is the joy of the person with the **Gift of Prophesy**.

○ We are all told to comfort others (1 Thessalonians 5:11), which is the joy of the person with the **Gift of Mercy**.

○ We are all told to do practical things for others (Galatians 5:13-14), which is the joy of the person with the **Gift of Ministry**.

○ We are all told to encourage and build up one another (Hebrews 10:24), which is the joy of the person with the **Gift of Exhortation**.

Though God wants us to work at manifesting the qualities of each of the *Gifts* that does not change the fact we only have one *Gift*. Each of us naturally finds greater joy manifesting one aspect of Christ's character because of our *Gift*. We must keep our focus on that, while working at manifesting the other six, with God's help.

What Types of Gifts Are There?

As every man hath received **the gift**, even so minister the same one to another, as good stewards of the manifold grace of God. If any man **speak**, let him speak as the oracles of God; if any man **minister**, let him do it as of the ability which God giveth: that God in all things may

> be glorified through Jesus Christ, to whom be praise and
> dominion for ever and ever. Amen.
>
> 1 Peter 4:10-11

Though there are **Seven Different Spiritual Gifts**, it seems
they fall into **Two Categories**. 1 Peter 4:10-11, tells us there are
Speaking Gifts and there are *Serving Gifts*.

- **Speaking Gifts** - *if any man speak.*
  Some gifts have a perspective with an emphasis on
  saying something.

- **Serving Gifts** - *if any man minister (serve).*
  Some gifts have a perspective with an emphasis
  on *doing* something.

Both *Categories of Gifts* complement each other. Too often,
those with *Speaking Gifts* wonder why those with *Serving Gifts*
do not speak out more. In addition, those with *Serving Gifts*
wonder why those with *Speaking Gifts* do not pitch in and do
more besides just talk. We must try to understand the *perspective*
of those with a different *Spiritual Gift* than ours and learn to
accept them for who they are.

What Are The Gifts?
Romans 12:7-8

Now we will look at each of the *Seven Spiritual Gifts*. Each
Gift is different from the others. Each one relates to a part of the
Body of Christ (Romans 12:4-6).

Our *Spiritual Gift* determines what part of the body we are.
It makes us *who* and *what we are*. Our *Gift* gives us a unique
perspective on life and the *potential* for service. It *motivates us*.

In many ways, the *Gifts* are like seven different *Personality
Types*. Each one has its own way of looking at life and relating
to others. Each has its own *motivations*, strengths and
weaknesses.

The following is a brief *description* of each *Gift*, followed
by a *possible interpretation*, based on that description and on

personal observations, of how each *Gift* functions in the life of an individual.

The Scripture tells us each *Gift* is like a specific part of the body. The Bible does not list which *Gift* corresponds to which part. The connection made here is only a suggestion.

1.   Giving

The word *Giving*, is the translation of the Greek word, **metadidous**. It means *one that imparts*.

We often think of the *Giver* as one who gives money. The word giving means to impart. It does not limit that imparting to money. The person with the *Gift of Giving* does not just focus on giving money. People with the *Gift of Giving* find their greatest joy in giving of themselves. They may give their *resources* or give their *ideas*.

The person with this *gift* may not like to speak before crowds, but they need to speak with someone, often with those in leadership, to give their ideas so they can be acted on. They must open their mouth to give those ideas to others.

The person with the *Gift of Giving* is often an originally creative person. They *listen* for needs, and then they come up with great ideas to help meet those needs.

Though the *Giver* can come up with the idea, they often are not good at getting all the details together, or at getting the idea implemented. They would much rather come up with the ideas or give the resources, have them appreciated, and then let others take care of organizing the ideas, or utilizing the resources, and carrying them out. That is why they work well with *Rulers*. *Rulers* take their ideas and organize them.

The *Giver* can usually work well in administration. They help keep the work going forward with new ideas and by providing the resources to carry on the work. They usually do not work as well in management because they are more of a thinking and conceptual person, than a people person.

Someone with the *Gift of Giving* may not have large monetary resources, though often they do. One reason many *Givers* have the resources is because the ideas they have often work in both a secular and spiritual context.

In the secular world, these people usually play a vital part as idea people in organizations and corporations. I knew one *Giver,* whose job, with a major technology company, was to come up with ideas to make the company money. One good idea each year could earn his company millions of dollars. The world sees the importance of that role, so must the church.

The *Serving Gifts* may have a hard time understanding how coming up with ideas and giving one's resources can be considered a *Spiritual Gift*. They often want the *Giver* to do more, like them.

Givers usually get along well with *Exhorters*. The *Exhorter* completes the ideas the *Giver* conceives. When they see their ideas acted on that inspires them to share more ideas.

We had a *Giver,* in one church I was in, who like most *Givers* was misunderstood. His creative thinking went over the heads of most people. Others would not take the time to listen to him. They wanted to see him more involved in practical areas of ministry in the church. I learned to appreciate his *Gift,* accepted him for who he was and encouraged him to use his *Gift.* One-on-one he would open up and share his insights and ideas with me. Those ideas helped me minister more effectively. As a result, he gave generously of his resources to help the ministry go forward.

Many times in my life, after hearing the ideas a *Giver* has, which are usually so good, I feel like saying, now why didn't I think of that?

The Giver's Areas of Weakness:

Romans 12:8, tells the *Giver* to give with simplicity. *Givers* tend to be too complicated.

If the *Giver* does not see people acting on their ideas, or using their resources wisely, they have a tendency to shut down, and withhold their ideas and resources.

The *Giver* may have a tendency to try to use their resources to manipulate people to accept, or to implement their ideas.

They must learn to trust the Lord and give with simplicity,

as He instructed, and leave the *Results* to God.

Possible Part of the Body: Ears

Givers are usually listening for needs. Then they try to come up with creative means of meeting those needs.

2.   Ruling

The word *Ruling*, is the translation of the Greek word, **proistamenous**. It means *one that takes the lead*. The person with the *Gift of Ruling* finds their real joy in keeping the overview.

The *Rulers* ability to see the overview, *the big picture,* usually helps them see the way things should work, which helps them organize and lead others.

Though the *Ruler* does not usually come up with original ideas, they have an unusual ability to grasp various ideas and concepts. They are good at taking the ideas from the *Giver* and *outlining* them in a workable format, and then *coordinating* their implementation.

The person with this *Gift of Ruling* usually is not a detailed person. They know the importance of details and draw on detailed people, like *Teachers*, to provide the information they need. Details would bog down the *Ruler* and keep them from maintaining the oversight and overall perspective they need. Being able to keep that oversight can help the *Ruler* work well in administration.

The *Ruler* is usually frustrated unless they can be *coordinating* something. They need to be in a position where they can keep the oversight, so they can be sure everything is working well. They are not happy doing any job, which keeps them from seeing what is happening.

I knew one *Ruler* who was very frustrated washing dishes at a church supper. While this person was *stuck in the kitchen washing dishes* (their words), a program was going on in another part of the building. This person was constantly wondering if the program was going as planned but could not see what was happening, nor could they do anything about it, hence the frustration. That situation would not have bothered a person with the Gift of *Ministry*.

The *Ruler* is one of those people who need to *speak*, to exercise their *Gift*. They need to let others know what the plan is and what needs to be done.

Rulers usually work well with *Teachers*. The *Teachers* do the research and get the details the *Rulers* need for their plans.

The *Ruler* likes to see things go the way they planned. They usually have more joy planning and organizing something, than in actually doing the job, unless they are actually leading others through the plan.

The Ruler's Areas of Weakness:

Romans 12:8, tells the *Ruler* to rule with diligence. Apparently, *Rulers* have a tendency to slack off.

The *Ruler* has a tendency to get bogged down with all that needs to be done. They can get so overwhelmed by all the details in all there is to do.

They usually want things to go the way they planned. This causes them to get frustrated with people or things, which interfere with their plans. They can have a hard time with people who change their plans.

If a *Ruler* meets resistance, or feels a job is not going the way they think it should, it is not unusual for them to try to do a job all by themselves. That way they can be sure things go the way they planned.

Possible Part of the Body: Eyes

Rulers are always looking to see things function smoothly. They think they must keep the big picture in view.

3.   Teaching

When most people think of teaching, they usually think of the *Ministry of Teaching*, rather than the *Gift of Teaching*. That causes a lot of confusion and makes people think they are not *Teachers*.

The Greek word, *didaskon*, translated *teacher,* in our English Bible, comes from the root word, *learner.* A *Teacher* is one whose *greatest joy is learning.*

In this context, it indicates *one who gathers information and then shares it with others.* That does not mean they have to be able to stand up in front of a crowd to do the imparting. Sometimes they do it in front of a group, sometimes by writing other times they do it one-on-one.

Teachers have a *Serving Gift.* Usually they would rather do the studying and research and have someone else do the speaking.

Teachers are usually extremely detailed people. Their greatest joy is studying and compiling facts and information. If they could spend a whole day studying, they would consider that a great day. They usually love books more than they do people.

Teachers usually work well with *Rulers* because a *Ruler* gives them an outline they can research and then fill in the details.

The *Teacher* is able to conceptualize truths. They are good at grasping complex ideas. Though they know, what they believe and why, sometimes they have a tendency to confuse others with their long detailed explanations. One reason they find it difficult to reduce their research down to a concise statement is because they believe all truth is important and all facts should be presented.

Teachers are very good at presenting both sides of an issue fairly. They usually provide more than enough information to identify each side's position. They believe the body of information will identify the correct position.

Teachers usually present an extremely well documented detailed presentation. If you are considering purchasing something, a *Teacher* is a great one to assign the task of finding the best buy. They will do extensive research and come up with all the details you need to make a good decision.

Teachers will rarely explain something from the Bible, like the Gospel, with just a few verses. They do not think a brief explanation does justice to the facts. They are good at showing you one hundred reasons why you should be saved.

I will never forget going on church visitation with a *Teacher*. Whenever he presented the Gospel, he started in Genesis and went all the way through to Revelation. I never saw him present the Gospel in less than an hour. He wanted to present *all* the facts so people could make a proper decision.

The *Teacher* can work well in management because they love to find the information needed and provide the details, which help get a job done.

Teachers usually do not get excited about physical work. They feel they can be used more effectively doing research and gathering information.

The Teacher's Areas of Weakness:

Romans 12:7, tells the *Teacher* to teach. Too often *Teachers* will study and accumulate information, but will not share it with others.

The *Teacher* has to beware their accumulation of information does not make them think they are better than others. They sometimes have a tendency to get puffed up and talk down to others.

They also have a tendency to give a person more information than that some people may want.

Possible Part of the Body: Mind

Teachers love to think about things and gather as much information as possible.

4.   Prophesy

The word *Prophesy* is the translation of the Greek word, **propheteian**. *Prophesy* is one of those words in Scripture, which appear in each of the lists in the *Outline on Spiritual Gifts*. It can be a *Gift*, a *Ministry* or a *Result*. Each one is different. The meaning must be determined by the context.

In the Old Testament, *Prophets* were primarily mouthpieces to *forth-tell* (tell others) God's truths. Some also *fore-told* (told in advance) the truth. When many people hear the word *Prophet*, they think of the *foretelling* aspect.

God used some *Prophets* in the Old Testament to deliver His inspired Word directly from God to people. That is not the meaning of the word in the context of *Spiritual Gifts* in the New Testament. The word *Prophet*, in this context, takes on its basic meaning of *one who proclaims the truth*.

The *Prophet* focuses on *logic*, and is concerned about *right and wrong*. *Prophets* can usually identify if something is wrong *(small or large)*, and comes up with a solution to correct it, even if the solution is not completely thought out.

Prophesy is a *Speaking Gift*. If the *Prophet* cannot speak, they will be frustrated. The person with the *Gift of Prophesy* enjoys persuading others.

All the *Prophets* I have met, usually notice if things are not correct. They notice if your tie is crooked. There is a good chance they will come up to you and mention it, or start to straighten it out themselves. They also notice if you say, or do something they believe is wrong, and usually point that out to you.

Prophets were not too popular in the Old Testament (Matthew 23:37). They always seemed to call for change. Many *Prophets* have that same problem today. When they see what they perceive to be a problem, they feel they have to say something. Sometimes they are too blunt or too direct in their approach. That can cause people to view them as pushy, perfectionists, or as legalistic. That causes some of those with other *Gifts*, not to want to be around them.

Prophets want facts and details so they can know they are proclaiming the truth, though they may not use many facts in their presentation. Sometimes they selectively use facts to convince others of the validity of their position. *Prophets* usually work well with *Teachers* because a *Teacher* gives them the facts they need so they can persuade people of the truth.

The *Prophet* has a hard time understanding why others do not see the truth as clearly as he does or she does. They often think others are deliberately ignoring it.

Prophets usually do not like presenting two sides to an issue. They wonder why people want to waste time looking at the wrong side. If they present two sides to an issue, they usually do it in such a way as to focus on the weaknesses of the other side and convince others of the strength, or logic, of their side.

The *Prophet* can be a good *initiator*. They want people to do right. They will try to convince others not to just know the truth but to act on it.

With some training in how to be more tolerable of others, the *Prophet* can work well in management. Many *Prophets* become lawyers or politicians.

The Prophets Areas of Weakness:

Romans 12:6, tells the *Prophet* to prophesy according to the proportion of faith. *Prophets* tend to either hold back, or go too far.

The *Prophet* has a tendency to get indignant when others do not respond to the Truth.

They tend to react too quickly to what they view as opposition to truth. They have to be careful they do not tear people down.

They need to make sure they are not insensitive, as they seek to persuade people to change.

A *Prophet* can be a good people person, but they have to work hard at it.

Possible Part of the Body: Mouth

Prophets usually feel they have to speak out. You will often find them telling somebody something.

5.   Mercy

The word *Mercy* is the translation of the Greek word, **heleon**. It means *to withhold something negative, which someone deserves.*

The person with the *Gift of Mercy* is a comforter, *someone who does not want to see people suffer*. They are concerned about people's feelings.

The *Mercy Person* often views people as victims. They

are even willing to show mercy to those whom others do not believe deserve mercy. Their greatest joy is seeing people's emotional needs are met.

The person with the *Gift of Mercy* helps to create an atmosphere for service. They are concerned about people's feelings.

The *Mercy Person* usually gets along well with people with the *Gift of Ministry*. They help provide comfort and emotional support to those *Ministry* People who serve others. *Mercy People* find satisfaction in the fact Servers help meet needs in other people's lives.

The person with the *Gift of Mercy* is a real server. They do not serve for the same reason as the person with the *Gift of Ministry*. They serve with one thing in mind, the needs and feelings of others.

The *Mercy Person* is usually not afraid to get their hands dirty, if that is what is needed to comfort and meet the needs of others.

Mercy People often find themselves involved in relief and social work. They like practical expressions, which directly affect the lives of others. They would rather work in the Nursery than clean the church, because of the direct people involvement.

The *Mercy Person* and *Prophet* should work well together but usually have the hardest time understanding and getting along with each other. One day I was teaching on this topic in a church and noticed a disturbance in the Deaf section. Two of the Deaf interrupted the interpreter and started to have an argument about what I was saying. This was especially distracting to me because I know Sign Language and knew what they were saying. The interpreter got them to sit down and wait for the end of the service to talk with me.

After the service, we had an interesting discussion. The one Deaf person said they thought the other Deaf person was not saved because of the way that person was always so coarse with other people. It seemed the second person was always correcting others. The second Deaf person felt the first one was not saved because the first person always seemed to overlook sin and wrong in people's lives and was primarily concerned about comforting others.

They were surprised to learn what they saw in the other person was a *Spiritual Gift* being manifested. One had the *Gift of Prophesy* and the other the *Gift of Mercy*. That understanding transformed their relationship.

The *Prophet* identifies the wrong in people's lives, the *Mercy Person* helps provide comfort and emotional support as the person deals with the changes they need to make. Rather than conflicting with each other, the *Prophet* and *Mercy Person* should perfectly complement each other.

The Mercy Person's Areas of Weakness:

Romans 12:8, tells the *Mercy Person* to be more cheerful. *Mercy People* tend to get moody and depressed too easily.

The Person with the *Gift of Mercy*, tends to get too involved in other people's problems and feelings, and sometimes breaks down under the load.

Surprisingly, *Mercy People* can be very unmerciful with a person they believe does not care about others.

Possible Part of the Body: Heart

The *Mercy Person* focuses a lot on feelings and meeting needs in other people's lives. They usually have a lot of heart.

6.   Ministry

The word *Ministry* is the translation of the Greek word, **diakonian**. *Ministry* is another one of those words, which has different shades of meaning, which must be determined by its context. We are all called to *Minister*. There is even an office within the Local Church, called *Deacons*, which is translated from the same Greek word. The Deacon's Ministry is to serve the physical needs of the church, which is different from the *Spiritual Gift of Ministry*.

The person with the *Gift of Ministry*, (The Server, The Doer) is *one whose real joy comes from doing practical things for others*. They are the ultimate servers. If there is a job to do, they will usually be there to get it done. Their joy is more in the *doing* of the task, than in its *completion*.

The *Server* is a detailed person because they need enough information so they can do a job properly.

Because a *Server* is a detailed person, they can get busy with the details of a job and put hours into doing something, which when they are finished, others may not see.

I know *Servers* who spend hours on projects around the home. When their spouse comes home, the spouse does not see the results of the hours of work and may ask the question, *What did you do today?* That greatly frustrates the *Server*.

Servers easily devote too much time and energy to one project to the exclusion of others. They do not intend to exclude other projects; they just believe what they find to do is important and end up giving too much time to one thing.

A *List of Things to Do* can help the *Server* see the various things they need to do and help them maintain balance. Asking a *Server* to clean the *church*, without giving them a list of what needs to be done, will be frustrating to them and to you. They will find many things to clean, which you never thought of, and may devote most of their time to those items, leaving the other items you want done, left undone.

Servers often find themselves serving in a variety of positions, even administrative ones, which they would rather not do, but they will do the job because it needs to be done.

Though *Servers* love to serve, I found many times *Servers* will not volunteer for a job, they would like to do. That may sound contrary to their *Gift* but it is not. You have to see their perspective on this to understand their reasoning. When a *Server* sees a job, they see the joy they would have in doing it. Often they will not volunteer for a job because they do not want to rob someone else of the joy of doing the job. They may not realize the person doing the job would much rather be doing something else. This is one reason you have to enlist personally some *Servers*.

You must acknowledge the work a **Servers** does. They do not serve to be seen, but they need to know people appreciate the work they do. All people need recognition but too often many of the tasks the *Server* does go unnoticed.

Servers are usually very dependable people. Some of the most encouraging and reliable people I have ever ministered with are *Servers*.

Servers usually get along well with *Mercy People*. The *Mercy People* are there to comfort the *Server* when they get tired or discouraged.

Servers also get along well with *Exhorters*. By doing their job, they encourage the *Exhorters*, whose joy is encouraging others and seeing a job completed. The *Exhorters* in turn come alongside, encourage the Servers, and make them feel like what they are doing is important.

The Servers Areas of Weakness:

Romans 12:7, tells the *Server* to, *wait on our ministering.* They are exhorted to stick with the job they are supposed to be doing.

Being such detailed people; *Servers* have a tendency to get sidetracked by the many details they encounter in a job.

The person with this *Gift of Ministry* seems to have the tendency to do too much and to focus on the job rather than on people.

If they feel they are doing too much, and not being appreciated, they will often close down and stop doing anything for a while.

Possible Part of the Body: Hands

Servers are like the hands. Their greatest joy is doing something practical for God.

7.   Exhortation

The word *Exhortation* is the translation of the Greek word, **parakalon**. It means *one called alongside someone to help or encourage.*

The *Exhorter* is *one whose greatest joy is stimulating the faith of others.* The *Exhorter* wants to see people encouraged and a job completed.

This *Gift* appears to be both a *Speaking Gift* and *Serving Gift*, at the same time. The *Exhorter* will often come alongside and work with others because they view this as necessary to get the job done. They also can be good at saying things to motivate others to get involved or to continue the work. They make other people want to get a job done.

People usually like being around the *Exhorter* because they find encouragement from the *Exhorter*.

The *Exhorter* is not as detailed as the *Server* is but they work well together. The *Exhorter* encourages the *Server* because they can see the joy of completing the task.

The person with this *gift* is often *very results oriented*. If they do not see results for their efforts, they can feel devastated.

Exhorters, who are in teaching and preaching ministries, tend to look for an outward response to gauge the effectiveness of their ministry. They look for people to respond. If they do not sense a response, they feel like they have failed. They are not like the *Prophet* whose joy is the proclamation. The *Exhorters* joy is the *response.*

Givers usually like *Exhorters* because the *Exhorter* encourages them, acts on the *Giver's* ideas, and utilizes the *Giver's* resources to accomplish things.

The *Exhorter* will often do whatever needs to be done to encourage others, and get a job done. They will organize, try to convince others, comfort others and do the job, though none of that is their primary joy.

The Exhorters Areas of Weakness:

Romans 12:8, tells the *Exhorter* to exhort. *Exhorters* are like *Servers* in that they have a tendency to get sidetracked. Instead of encouraging others, too often they get involved doing the job. They need to train and encourage others instead of doing the job themselves.

The person with the *Gift of Exhortation* has a tendency to do more than they should in their quest to encourage others and to get the job done.

The *Exhorter* feels they must always be moving toward a goal. Sometimes they do not enjoy their successes because they are pressing on too hard. They have a tendency to run down and wear out.

Possible Part of the Body: Feet

The *Exhorter* is like the feet, they try to take the body where they think it needs to go.

The Interrelation of the Gifts

When all the *Gifts* are exercised in a church, the result is a growing and smoothly functioning body (Ephesians 4:15-16).

Notice the flow in the following illustration, of one way the *Gifts* can interrelate with one another:

> The **Giver** *comes up with an idea and presents it to the Ruler. The* **Ruler** *puts together an overview of how the idea could work and gives that to the Teacher. The* **Teacher** *takes the overview, researches it and fills it in with details. The* **Prophet** *takes the idea, and the information gathered by the Teacher, and convinces others of the validity and importance of the idea. The* **Mercy Person** *balances the somewhat forceful presentation of the Prophet and helps create an atmosphere for service and offers emotional support for those who will help implement the idea. The* **Server** *takes the idea and puts it into action. The* **Exhorter** *then comes along and provides practical encouragement, which helps others complete the task.*

Notice how well the *Gifts* can work together. Each *Gift* approached the idea with a different *perspective*, but they all worked together to bring the idea from inception to completion.

Each person needs to exercise their own *Spiritual Gift* and learn how to relate with the other *Gifts*. This will result in churches, which glorify God. The interrelation between the *Gifts* not only helps a church. This can help any organization, business or government, which understands how it works.

Difficulties Identifying Your Gift

Many people want to identify their *Spiritual Gift*. I tell them, it is not as important to understand *what* your specific *Gift* is, as it is to understand you have a unique *perspective* on life, which gives you a special *potential* for service.

Some people, who hear a teaching like this, try to identify other people's *Gifts*. That is not always possible to do successfully. Though certain *Gifts* tend to *function* in certain ways, the *Gift* is *who we are*, not *what we do*. Just because someone does something effectively, and manifests the characteristics of a certain *Gift*, does not mean that is their *Gift*. What you see may not be their joy at all; they may be working very hard, with the help of the Holy Spirit, to manifest that characteristic, in obedience to the Lord's command.

The important thing is to realize different people have different *perspectives* because of their *Spiritual Gift*. We must accept them for who they are and learn to relate to them.

The following factors sometimes make it difficult to determine your specific *Spiritual Gift*:

O   Incorrect interpretation as to what are, and are not, *Spiritual Gifts*. If you think something is a *Gift* and it is not, or do not know something is a *Gift*, you will not know what your *Gift* is.

O   When you try to live up to other people's expectations and try to be what they think you should be, rather than what God wants you to be.

O   When someone else does not do their part and you try to fill in for them and then confuse what you *do*, with who you really *are*.

O   The longer you are saved, and allow the Holy Spirit to develop the other characteristics in your life, you or others, may lose sight of your basic perspective. That is not a problem for you, but it may confuse others who are trying to figure out what your *Gift* is.

The Unbeliever and Spiritual Gifts

I believe everyone has a *Spiritual Gift*, including non-believers. Please read on to see what I mean.

> And the very God of peace sanctify you wholly; and I pray God your whole spirit and soul and body be preserved blameless unto the coming of our Lord Jesus Christ.   1 Thessalonians 5:23

The Bible tells us in 1 Thessalonians 5:23, we are all made up of a body, soul and spirit. That applies to all of us, saved or unsaved.

Before we are saved, we are all spiritually dead. That does not mean we do not have a spiritual part to us. Spiritual death, in the Bible, refers to *separation from God*. It implies a defect and inability to function properly. When we are saved, the Holy Spirit removes the separation and makes us spiritually alive. He regenerates us. I believe that regeneration involves giving new life to our *Spiritual Gift*. It opens our eyes *(our perspective, our gift)* which were darkened and gives them life (Acts 26:18; Ephesians 1:18).

> To open their eyes, and to turn them from darkness to light, and from the power of Satan unto God, that they may receive forgiveness of sins, and inheritance among them which are sanctified by faith that is in me.
>   Acts 26:18

> The eyes of your understanding being enlightened...
>   Ephesians 1:18

I have seen the perspective of the different *gifts* manifested in the lives of many unsaved people. Because their eyes *(gift)* are darkened *(spiritually dead)*, this becomes a major point of frustration for them. They do not have a clear perspective on what God wants them to do and cannot utilize their full potential, without the *Indwelling of the Holy Spirit*.

If these deductions are correct, understanding what *Spiritual Gift* an unsaved person has can be helpful in attempting to relate the Gospel to them. Though their *Gift* is not fully functional, because it is separated from God and needs new life, understanding the basic strengths and weaknesses of each *Gift* can help you understand them.

Different Ways Unsaved People Look at the Gospel:

O   **Unsaved Givers** - tend to respond to the wonderful gift of eternal life God unselfishly gave for us and the opportunity He wants to give us to share that gift with others.

O   **Unsaved Rulers** - tend to respond to the concept God has a plan for the ages and a plan for each of our lives. They love the order and organization God can bring to their life.

O   **Unsaved Teachers** - tend to respond to the overwhelming body of evidence, which supports the Scriptures. They are fascinated at all the facts and information in the Bible.

O   **Unsaved Prophets** - tend to respond to the truth of the Gospel. They need to be convinced it is the truth. They enjoy the idea of convincing others of its truths.

O   **Unsaved Mercy People** - tend to respond to the love of God. They need to see God is Love and we need His help to love others more effectively.

O   **Unsaved Servers** - tend to respond to the fact, God has a special place of service for them and that their service can make a difference.

O   **Unsaved Exhorters** - tend to respond to the completeness they see in Christ. They like the idea they can help encourage others with the Gospel and make a visible difference.

There is much more which can be said about this concept. I address that in more depth in another book, *Understanding People By Their Spiritual Gift.*

Conclusion

It is important to understand everyone has a specific *Spiritual Gift.* That *Gift* gives us a unique *perspective* on life, which is different from others and gives us *potential* for service.

We must learn to accept the different perspective others have, and then learn how to work together to glorify God.

In the next chapter, we will look at the various *Ministries* God gives where we can exercise our *Spiritual Gift.*

CHAPTER THIRTEEN
QUESTIONS

Verse to Memorize: Romans 12:6-8

13.1   What is the warning we are given in Romans 12:3?

13.2   How many *Spiritual Gifts* are there?

13.3   How many *Spiritual Gifts* does each person have?

13.4   What are the two categories of *Gifts*?

13.5   Briefly describe each of the *Gifts of the Spirit*.

QUESTIONS FOR ADDITIONAL THOUGHT

13.6   Discuss the context, preceding the listing of the *Gifts of the Spirit*, in Romans 12:6-8.

13.7   Discuss how the proper functioning of each of the *Gifts of the Spirit* would enhance your *ministry*.

13.8   Discuss the reasoning and practical ramifications of the concept that the unsaved have a *Spiritual Gift*.

CHAPTER FOURTEEN

The Gifts of the Holy Spirit
The Ministries

Two Types of Ministries

In this chapter, we are going to look at the third part of the Outline relating to *Spiritual Gifts*. First, we looked at the *Operations*; the *Results* God sovereignly gives as we use our *Gift* for Him. Then we looked at the *Gifts* God gives. The *Gifts* give us a unique *perspective* on life and the *potential* for service. Now we will look at the *Administrations* (Ministries).

As we saw earlier in this book, the word *Administrations* means *Ministries*. The *Ministries* are specific areas of service where we put our *Spiritual Gift* into action. Remember the *Gifts* focus on what we *are* and what *motivates* us. The *Ministries* focus on what we *do*.

As we look at the *Ministries*, one of the most important things to understand is, *any Spiritual Gift* can be used in a variety of *Ministries*.

Too often people stereotype the *Gifts* and relegate some of them to one or two particular *Ministries*. God does not limit us the way man does. He can use *any Gift* in *any Ministry* so it will be a blessing to both those being ministered to and those doing the *Ministry*.

Some people think the person best suited for the *Ministry of Teaching* would be someone with the *Gift of Teaching*. I discovered that might not be the case at all. In fact, most of the best *Teachers* I ever sat under had a different *Gift* than the *Gift of Teaching*.

It is important to remember the *Gifts* have to do with *motivation*, not *function*. The *Gifts* give us a *perspective* and *potential* for service.

For example, though some *Gifts* have greater joy teaching than others, God can use any of the *Gifts* in a *Teaching Ministry*.

A Look at How Each Gift Can Do the Ministry of Teaching:

O   The **Giver**, would teach from the perspective of giving one's self and resources to God.

O   The **Ruler** would teach from the perspective of keeping the overview of a particular subject. *Rulers* usually teach from an outline, rather than from detailed notes.

O   The **Teacher** would teach giving all of the details. They would try to present all the facts related to a topic.

O   The **Prophet** would teach from the perspective of contrasting right and wrong. They would focus more on what they felt was right.

O   The **Mercy Person** would teach focusing on making sure the material somehow met a need or provided comfort to those instructed.

O   The *Server* would teach because someone needed to do the job. They would focus on practical ways to serve God.

O   The *Exhorter* would teach in a way that focused on encouraging others to apply the truth so the work of God would be completed.

Our *Spiritual Gift* gives the *perspective*, our *Ministry* gives the *platform* to express that perspective. Though our *Spiritual Gift* does not change, God may change the *Ministry* where we use it. No one has to serve in one ministry for all of his or her life.

We need to determine prayerfully what God wants accomplished at each point in our lives. Then we need to use our *Gift* in whatever *Ministry* God gives us for that time in our life. One of the beauties of the *Gifts* is we are not locked into one *Ministry* all our lives. Each *Spiritual Gift* can be used effectively in almost any *Ministry*. As illustrated above with the *Ministry of Teaching*.

As we seek to determine which *Ministry* God has for us, it is important to recognize there are *Two Different Categories of Ministries*. Some are given to be used *Within the Local Church* and some are given to be used on a broader scale, those ministries are given *To the Churches*. It appears both of these are complete listings or ministries in specific passages in the Word of God. Each of the *Ministries*, listed in both contexts, are *Specific Types of Ministries*. Each *Type of Ministry* has various ways it can be conducted.

Ministries to the Churches
Ephesians 4:11-16

And He gave some **apostles**; and some **prophets**; and some, **evangelists**; and some, **pastors** and **teachers**.

Ephesians 4:11

The *Ministries to the Churches*, are *Ministries* God gives, with the intention of having them used by more than one church. They are listed in Ephesians 4:11. Though a person with one of these *Ministries* may remain in one church for an extended period of time, they must be willing to let God move them to another church, if He so directs.

The *Ministries to the Churches* are *Ministries*, which usually serve as an *occupation* for a person. Those serving in these *Ministries* are often referred to as those in *full-time Christian service*. In one sense, that is a misnomer because all Christians are in full-time Christian service. Perhaps a better way to classify these *Ministries* is to refer to them as, the *Professional Ministries to the Churches*.

Those with these *Ministries* usually serve more than one Local Church in their life. Some people, in these *Ministries*, serve more than one church simultaneously.

The *Ministries to the Churches* are *Five Different Categories of Ministry*. Each Local Church should both utilize, and support financially and with prayer, *Ministries* in each of these five areas so every area of the work of God is supported. Any *Ministries* the church is considering to utilize, or support, should be evaluated to be sure it falls under one of these five areas, listed in Ephesians 4:11.

1.   Apostles

The word *Apostle* was not translated in this verse. It is the transliteration of the Greek word, **apostolos**. This is one of those Greek words that has a variety of meanings. The specific meaning of a word must be determined by the context of the passage.

The word **apostolos** is very similar in meaning to the Greek word, **angelos**. Both words were used in everyday language and had non-religious as well as religious significance. Though they are similar, they are also distinct.

The primary meaning of the word **angelos**, is a *messenger*. Yet it also has a spiritual significance in many passages, where it is translated *angel*. In those cases, it refers to a heavenly messenger from God.

The word **apostolos**, which is translated *apostle*, carries the meaning of *one who is sent forth with **authority** and with a message*. **Apostolos** goes a step further than a messenger *(angelos)* does, in that the *apostle* not only carries a message but also has authority.

Some eliminate this area of *Ministry* by reserving this word for the original twelve *Apostles* of Christ. It is true, the Twelve Disciples were also called *Apostles*. It must be remembered, the word *Apostle,* was a common Greek word, which was used, in everyday language. In the Bible, *Apostle* was also used to refer to people other than the Twelve *Apostles*.

When the Apostle Paul explained who saw Christ, after the resurrection, he gave a list in 1 Corinthians 15:1-11. He identified *the Twelve,* at the beginning of the list. Then, toward the end of the list, he referred to another group as, *all the apostles.*

In Acts 15:6, Paul met with the *apostles,* at Jerusalem. In Galatians 1:19, Paul comments on that meeting and says he met Peter and James *(the half-brother of Jesus)*. He did not mention meeting with any of the other *Twelve Apostles*. The *Apostles* he met with must have included others than the original *Twelve Disciples.*

In 2 Corinthians 8:23, Paul identifies Titus, and the others serving with him in his traveling church planting work as, *the messengers (apostoloi) of the churches.*

Some other people referred to in the New Testament as *Apostles*, include Barnabas and Paul (Acts 14:14); Apollos (1 Corinthians 4:6-9); and possibly, Andronicus and Junia *(a woman)* (Romans 16:7). Epaphroditus is identified as, *your messenger (apostolon)*, in Philippians 2:25. He was a missionary *(apostle)* sent out by the Philippians.

Jesus is called, *the Apostle* in Hebrews 3:1. He was the ultimate missionary.

Apostles rightly defined in the context of Ephesians 4:11, are a valid and necessary *Ministry* for today. They are usually known as Missionaries or Church Planters. In this context, they are ones *sent out from a Local Church* to carry the message of Christ, with authority, to a *different* geographic area. Their emphasis is usually on starting or strengthening churches.

2.   Prophets

Prophet is another transliterated Greek word. The Greek word is **prophetas**. In Scripture it refers to, *one who proclaims the Word of God.*

This is another *Ministry*, some eliminate, claiming it is not valid for today. They view a *Prophetic Ministry* as having the same characteristics as some of the *Old Testament Prophets*, who directly delivered God's Word to man.

It is true *some Prophets* in the Old Testament were used to give man the inspired Word of God but they did not *all* do that. Some *Prophets* just *proclaimed* God's Word.

Trying to define the role of a *Prophet* as one who only gives the direct inspired Word of God is a misunderstanding of this important *Ministry*.

Some **Old Testament Prophets** proclaimed God's Word but did not give the inspired Word of God to man. That included: Gad (1 Samuel 22:5), Nathan (2 Samuel 7:2), Ahijah (1 Kings

11:29), Iddo (2 Chronicles 13:22), Oded (2 Chronicles 15:8), Elijah (1 Kings 18:22), and Elisha (2 Kings 6:12).

There were **Prophets in the New Testament** who proclaimed God's Word but did not give us the inspired Word of God. That included Agabus (Acts 21:10), some at Antioch (Acts 13:1), Judas and Silas (Acts 15:32), and some in Corinth (1 Corinthians 14).

Prophet was a common Greek word with a non-religious meaning. The common Greek usage was, *one who proclaimed a message to a particular group of people.*

The *Ministry of Prophet* today, in the context of Ephesians 4:11, is not one who gives man the inspired Word of God, but rather one who *proclaims* and *expounds* the already complete Word of God, in such a way God's people will understand it and respond to it.

As in the Old Testament, the *Prophet's* message today is *mainly to God's people.* Prophets today do not deliver new revelation from God to man. Now that we have the complete written Word of God to Man, the prophet's ministry focuses on directing God's people to truths *in* God's Word, truths they need to apply, to make a needed change in their lives. *Prophets* often do this through a pulpit ministry in various churches, *though* it is not limited to the pulpit.

Prophets are often mislabeled as *Evangelists. Evangelists* have a ministry, which is primarily to the unsaved. Though *Prophets* should preach the Gospel *(the good news of salvation),* their main ministry is to call on Christians to change and be revived. *Prophets*, have what we often refer to today, as a *Revival* ministry. They should be called *Revivalists,* not *Evangelists.*

3. Evangelists

The word Evangelist is another transliterated Greek word. The Greek word is **evangelistas**. It was another common Greek word. It means *one who proclaims good news.*

Most Bible scholars agree without question that the last three ministries in this passage, *Evangelists, Pastors* and *Teachers,* are all valid *Ministries* for today.

The *Evangelist* is one who proclaims the Gospel, the good news, primarily to the unsaved, by means of an *Evangelistic Ministry*.

Those with this *Ministry* may hold evangelistic crusades, conduct evangelistic programs on television or radio, produce and distribute evangelistic literature or conduct extensive personal evangelistic work.

Remember, *Evangelist*, like the others in this listing of *ministries*, is an *Area of Ministry to* various churches. *Evangelists* usually minister to many churches.

It is also important to understand there are some Christians who can be involved in this and other *Areas of Ministry*, as administrative and support personnel.

It is important to understand there are a variety of ways to express this, and the other *Ministries*. Someone could have an evangelistic writing ministry. Some have evangelistic music *ministries*. They may write evangelistic music, perform it, produce it or do all of these.

4. Pastors

The word *Pastor*, in this verse, is the Latin word meaning, *to pasture*. It refers to the *work* of the shepherd. The shepherd *pastured* the sheep.

Those with a *Pastoral Ministry* are *those who lead or comfort the sheep*. This includes what we refer to today as *Pastors*, as well as those with *Counseling Ministries*.

There is a big difference between being a *Pastor* and being a *Preacher* or *Bible Teacher*. Many in *Pastoral Ministries* preach and teach, but all Preachers and Teachers are not Pastors. Churches would do well to learn the difference.

The word, *Pastors*, used in Ephesians 4:11, focuses on, *pasturing the sheep*. Though a *Pastor* of a Church should be able to teach and preach, they absolutely must be one with a heart to *pasture* the people. Those who serve as a *Pastor* of a church must have a Pastor's heart. Those who want to preach or teach but do not have a Pastor's heart can serve in a variety of other *ministries.* You do not have to be a Great Preacher or Great Teacher to be a *Great Pastor.*

Pastors often work in one particular church at a time. Some remain in one church for an extended period of time, but many serve a number of *ministries* over the years. That is something God determines. Remember *Pastors* are one of those *Ministries* for more than one church.

Some churches have more than one *Pastor.* Some serve as a Youth Pastor or Music Pastor. Some with *Pastoral Ministries* work with other *Pastors*, or serve in a *Pastoral capacity* with a mission board or organization.

Pastoral Ministry does not necessarily mean *pastoring a church.* Though the Bible clearly teaches only certain men are to be the *Pastor* of a congregation (1 Timothy 3:1-7; Titus 1:6-9), women and other men may have other types of *Pastoral Ministries.*

Many *Pastoral Ministries* focus specifically on counseling. There is a great need for women in those *ministries.* Some people with *Counseling (Pastoral) Ministries* serve many churches at a time.

I wrote a comprehensive manual for churches called, *How to Find the Right Pastor.* Besides providing direction in finding a *Pastor*, that book includes a section, which shows the different way each of the *Seven Spirituals Gifts* would serve as a *Pastor.*

5.   Teachers

This is the only truly translated word in this verse. In this context, the *Teacher* is *one who is involved in instructing others in the Word of God.*

Some Bible scholars, usually *Teachers*, try to link the last two *Ministries* together as *Pastor-Teacher.* Though *Pastoral Ministry* often involves Teaching, a *Teaching Ministry* is different from a *Pastoral Ministry.* There are many valid *Teaching Ministries*, which are not *Pastoral.* It is best to retain the distinctions God gives and identify these as *two different Ministries. Pastors* do not have to call themselves Pastor-Teachers, to Teach.

Today, *Teachers* can serve churches in a variety of ways, such as Bible Teachers, Bible Conference Speakers, Christian School Teachers, Bible College & Seminary Teachers, and as Writers.

Ministries Within the Local Church

> And God hath set some **in the church**, first apostles, secondarily prophets, thirdly teachers, after that miracles, then gifts of healings, helps, governments, diversities of tongues. 1 Corinthians 12:28

The *Second Category of Ministries*, the Scriptures identify, are *Eight Ministries* to be exercised *within* one specific Local Church. These are listed in 1 Corinthians 12:28.

This passage was addressed to a Local Church, which was having a hard time identifying what was truly important in the spiritual realm. They were neglecting certain areas of *Ministry*. They focused mainly on the more prominent *Vocal Ministries*, which in their minds gave people spiritual status.

God had the Apostle Paul give them this *List of the Eight Ministries* God wants to see functioning in each Local Church. God wanted them, and us, to see that though some *Ministries* may be more prominent, and necessary at different times, each one is important.

A number of these *Ministries* are *similar* to the *Professional Ministries* identified in Ephesians 4:11, which God gave *to* be used among various churches. The difference is these *Ministries* specifically function *within* a particular Local Assembly.

These are *Areas of Ministry*. These eight seem to be a complete list of the different *Types of Ministries* each church should have.

Too many times, we are like the church at Corinth. We have our own ideas of what *Ministries* are more important and which ones we should have. If you ask people to list the most important *Ministries* a church should have many people will put a *Music Ministry* or *Youth Ministry* at the top of their list. It is interesting God does not include either of those in this *List of Ministries* He says a church should have. None of the epistles in the New Testament mentions anything about a specific Music or Youth Ministry.

Do not misunderstand this, God loves music and wants us to use music in ministry and He wants us to minister to youth. I believe those are important *ministries*. I served as a Youth Pastor and authored a book, *Becoming a Dynamic Youth Leader*. However, neither Music nor Youth Ministry are one of the *Eight Areas of Ministry* God says every church should have. To qualify as a *Valid Ministry* for a church, they must fall under one of the *Eight Areas of Ministry*.

It is a good idea for each church to look at this section to see if they have all the *Areas of Ministry* God says each church should have.

It is important again to note people with *different Spiritual Gifts* can serve in the *same Ministry*. *Different Gifts* bring their *unique perspective* to the *different Ministries*. The key is for each person to find a *place of Ministry*, in a Local Church, where they can effectively use their *Gift*.

Those who fulfill these particular *Ministries* are usually referred to as *Laymen*. It is possible some of these *Ministries* could become professional staff positions in a larger church, but that usually is not the case in medium sized or smaller churches.

It is also important to understand someone does not have to serve in one *Ministry* all his or her life. We need to be flexible and allow people to change *Ministries* from time to time. A person's *Gift* does not change but their *Ministry* may.

Either men or women can fulfill each of these *Ministries*, as long as you follow Biblical guidelines.

1. Apostles

Just like the *Apostles* to the various churches, these *Apostles*, are those who are *sent out from the church with a message*. The difference is these are still *in the church*.

How can you minister by going *out from* a church, yet still be *in* the church? These are the ones who work within the context of one Local Church, in the area of *Outreach and*

Evangelism. Those with this ministry are sent out by their church, into the community, with the goal of reaching others for Christ.

Some *Music Ministries* could fall under this *Area of Ministry*, if they are using music as an evangelistic outreach.

2.   Prophets

The word Prophet, in this context, has the same meaning as its use under the *Ministries to the Various Churches*, but here it is expressed in the context of the *Local Church*. This is a ministry of preaching and expounding the Word of God, *within* a Local Church, in such a way lives are changed.

This does not refer to the Pastor's specific preaching ministry but to a *preaching and expounding ministry* for others.

There can be many opportunities within a Local Church for this ministry of preaching and expounding the Word of God. This can involve preaching to various groups, such as: Teens, Children, Senior Saints, Singles, College and Career Groups, Men's Groups, Ladies Groups, at Special Meetings and any time preaching or expounding the Word of God is needed.

Some *Music Ministries* could fall under this Area of Ministry, if they are presenting the Word of God and calling on people to change.

3.   Teachers

This is a similar ministry to *the Ministry of Teaching to the Various Churches*, but this *Teaching Ministry* is exercised *within* the context of a *Local Church*.

This is the *Ministry of Christian Education* within the Local Church. There are many opportunities for a *Teaching Ministry in a Local Church.*

This Area of Ministry can include Sunday School Teachers, Bible Study Teachers, Disciplers, Youth Workers, Nursery Workers, Literacy Tutors and any other area, where *Teaching* can be used.

Some *Music Ministries* could fall under this *Area of Ministry*, if they are teaching the Word of God through music.

4.   Miracles

Some people would like to eliminate this as a valid *Ministry*. They confuse this with *signs* and *wonders* (Acts 2:22). This is different. Signs and wonders were given to confirm the Word of God and are not very common. *Miracles **(dunamis)*** are a ministry every church should have.

Miracles are one of the most neglected *ministries* within the Local Church. God wants to exercise His ***dunamis,*** miraculous *power* in the Local Church (Ephesians 3:14-21).

This is the *Ministry of challenging and enlarging the Faith and Vision of those in the church.* When properly exercised, this ministry helps create a dynamic, enthusiastic church.

This includes reaching out in ways God's *power* is clearly seen. Lives are miraculously changed, strongholds of Satan are broken and Christ is exalted.

5.   Gifts of Healings

This is another ministry some consider no longer valid. That is due to misunderstanding and misinterpretation. Notice this does not say the *Gift of Healing*, but rather the plural, *Gifts of Healings*.

This is the *Ministry, within the church, of helping others find Healing over and over again.* Though God sovereignly and miraculously heals people every day, there is a ministry of helping others find healing in a variety of ways.

This could refer to a *Medical Ministry*, within the church. It could also refer to a *Counseling Ministry*, which helps people heal from the inside out. There is a tremendous need for that type of ministry. People whose hearts are healed will often have some form of physical healing follow, even if it is unseen (Proverbs 17:22).

I ministered in churches in other lands who interpret this to mean the church should have a *Medical Ministry*. They have active health clinics, which help them, minister to hundreds they would never reach any other way. *Medical Missions* have always been very effective missions. Why has the church lost sight of how such an essential ministry could, and should be exercised by the Local Church? This helps give us a *Ministry to the total person.*

Some *Music Ministries* could fall under this A*rea of Ministry*, if they are comforting people and bring a healing touch to others.

6.   Helps

This is a very important area of ministry, which often is overlooked. This includes those involved in the *Technical and Support, Hands-on Ministries of the Local Church.* People with this *Ministry* usually use their hands and abilities to serve the Lord in physical ways.

There are many opportunities to be involved in this type of *Ministry.* Some opportunities include: care and maintenance of the church's facilities; building and expanding facilities; audio-visual ministries; radio and television; puppets; drama; music; ushers; parking lot attendants; bus drivers; meal and refreshment providers; and providing accommodations, just to name a few.

I have been in churches, which organized a number of their people in this area of *Ministry* and call them the *Helping Hand Ministry.* Sometimes these ministries provide food for the sick, other times they paint a house for a widow, and sometimes they provide clothing and disaster relief.

Some churches, particularly *Southern Baptists* and *Mennonites,* express this ministry with a Disaster Relief outreach or through other ministries such as *Habitat for Humanity.* Some do this in their own geographic area. Some go as groups, from their church, to help in other areas.

The opportunities for this type of service are almost unlimited, just like our God.

7.   Governments

This involves those who are involved in the daily administration *(governing)* of the Ministry of the church. God expects everything to be done decently and in order. Organizational and office type people help to coordinate and keep the ministry of the Local Church going forward.

There is a great need to have more people involved in this type of *Ministry*.

This *Area of Ministry* includes the directors of each ministry within the church, secretarial workers, and those who work with the church finances.

8.   Diversities of Tongues

This is another *Area of Ministry,* which some like to remove from their list. That is usually due to a misunderstanding of what this *Ministry* really means.

These are those involved in Linguistic Ministries and Cross-Cultural Communication within the Local Church. If we are ever going to fulfill the Great Commission and reach all people groups for the Lord (Matthew 28:19-20; Acts 1:8), we need more churches to implement these *Ministries*. This will help a church have a real missionary vision, right in its own community. This will also enable churches to prepare their own missionaries to send to the field.

People could help the task of world evangelization and discipleship, through this *Ministry*, by staying right within their own church. There is a tremendous need for Scriptures, training materials, curriculum, books, songbooks, and a whole host of printed materials to be translated into other languages. With all the technology available today, people who know other languages, or those who will learn them, could be actively involved in a translation project, through their own church, without having to leave and go to a mission field. What a tremendous way for a church to become more involved in missions.

This can also include a *Ministry* of teaching your national language to those who immigrated to your country. In the United States and parts of Canada, this would be a TESOL *(Teaching English to Speakers of Other Languages)* Ministry. Sometimes this is referred to as ESL *(English as Second Language)* Ministry. ESL is the proper name for this *Ministry* in another country, where English will be used as the second language.

Your Part and God's Part

Each of these *Ministries*, from both categories, is an area of spiritual service. We need the *Filling* and *Empowering of the Holy Spirit* to do them effectively.

Though God can intervene supernaturally in any of these *Areas of Ministry*, He *expects* us to work at learning skills to develop our effectiveness in the ministry where we serve.

If you are a *Teacher*, you need to learn how to research. If you are a Preacher *(prophet)*, you need to learn how to preach. If you have the *Ministry of Helps*, you must learn to be a better helper. If your Ministry is Linguistics *(Diversities of Tongues)*, you need to sharpen your language skills.

Do your preparation, then serve in the *power* of the Holy Spirit and allow God to give the *results*.

Conclusion

God wants every believer to have a *Ministry* where they can utilize their *Spiritual Gift*. We are to either serve in a *Ministry to Various Churches*, or find a place of *Ministry within a specific Local Church*.

Now that you have an understanding of the *Gifts of the Holy Spirit*, in the next chapter, we will look at the Pentecostal and Charismatic Movements and the impact they have had on people's understanding of this important doctrine.

CHAPTER FOURTEEN
QUESTIONS

Verses to Memorize: Ephesians 4:11-12

14.1   Which *Spiritual Gift* works best in which *Ministry*?

14.2   What are the *Two Categories of Ministries*?

14.3   What are the *Five Ministries To the Churches*?

14.4   What are the *Eight Ministries Within the Local Church*?

QUESTIONS FOR ADDITIONAL THOUGHT

14.5   How can the Local Church better utilize, support and encourage the *Five Ministries To the Churches*? What implications should this have on your church budget and missions giving?

14.6   How are, or how can, all *Eight Ministries for Within the Local Church* be implemented within your church?

CHAPTER FIFTEEN

The Pentecostal & Charismatic Movements

Brief Overview

To conclude our study, we will look more specifically at two different groups, which play a major role in the controversy over the Holy Spirit. Both groups identify themselves primarily in relation to their position on the Holy Spirit.

What comes to your mind, when you hear the words, *Pentecostal* or *Charismatic*? What picture do you get? Do you picture a quiet, reserved, unenthusiastic group of people? Probably not. For years, *Pentecostals* and *Charismatics* have been known for their enthusiastic spirit. These two groups impacted almost all of Christianity, in some way.

What comes to your mind, when you hear the phrase, *Speaking in Tongues?* If you picture someone using some type of ecstatic utterance, then those movements have influenced you, whether or not you agree with that concept.

What comes to your mind when you hear someone say, *they believe in healing?* Do you picture someone who went to the Church Health Clinic, or someone who found emotional healing through a Christian Counselor? Probably not. That is because of the influence of the *Pentecostal* and *Charismatic* movements.

These movements re-defined the way Christians think about certain terms used in the Bible. Those re-definitions have now become the standard definitions to many people.

It is important to understand *Pentecostals* and *Charismatics* are two different groups. They are similar in some ways, but each has their own distinctive views regarding the work of the Holy Spirit in the life of a believer. It is important to understand their differences.

Around the beginning of the twentieth century, there was the emergence of a particular segment of Christianity, which came to be known as the *Pentecostals*. Various denominations like the *Assemblies of God*, and other groups, have this heritage.

In the early 1960's, a different group, now known as the *Charismatics*, arose among old-line Protestant denominations. The *Charismatics* held very similar beliefs to the *Pentecostals*, but were not willing to separate from their own churches and do not accept all the teachings of the *Pentecostal* churches.

Another distinct group, calling themselves *Catholic Charismatics* arose in the Roman Catholic Church between 1966-1967.

The following briefly summarizes the distinctions between *Pentecostals* and the three different types of *Charismatics*:

1.   Pentecostals

Pentecostals are usually Gospel preaching groups, which emphasize salvation by faith in the finished work of Christ through His death, burial and resurrection.

Pentecostals usually teach believers need a separate work of the Holy Spirit subsequent to (*after*) salvation. This work of the Holy Spirit is often called *the Filling* or *Baptism of the Spirit*. Those who are truly *Pentecostal* believe speaking in ecstatic utterances is the evidence of this. They call that experience *Speaking in Tongues*.

Pentecostal groups include churches like *The Church of God, The Assemblies of God*, Holiness Groups and others.

2.   Charismatics (Neo-Pentecostals)

Many people mistakenly classify *Pentecostals* as *Charismatics*. Some *Pentecostals* do not object to being called *Charismatics*. Often, *Pentecostals* will try to draw people in from the *Charismatic Movement*. Though they are similar to *Pentecostals, Charismatics* are different.

Charismatics were originally called *Neo-Pentecostals*, which means the *New Pentecostals*. They share *some* of the same doctrinal beliefs as the *Pentecostals*, but there are differences. Some of the differences are very significant.

Charismatics are a very diverse group. In order to understand what a *Charismatic* believes, it is important to know which *Charismatic* group a person is from. Each group can mean something different when they say they are *Charismatic*:

O   **Evangelical Charismatics**

Evangelical Charismatics are from Gospel Preaching churches. They profess a crisis experience, with the Holy Spirit, subsequent to *(after)* the new birth. These often teach that experience with the Holy Spirit *can* be evidenced by speaking in ecstatic utterances, *or* some other outward manifestation.

Some *Evangelical Charismatics* do not teach an outward manifestation is necessary as evidence of this subsequent work of the Holy Spirit. That is a key doctrinal difference between a *Charismatic* and a *Pentecostal*.

Pentecostals teach *anyone* who truly has that subsequent work of the Holy Spirit *will* speak in ecstatic utterances. *Charismatics* teach *some* who have that subsequent work of the Holy Spirit *may* speak in ecstatic utterances.

O   **Liberal Charismatics**

Liberal Charismatics are individuals from Liberal Protestant Churches. Sometimes what they refer to as a *Charismatic* encounter is often what is actually a conversion experience. For the first time in their lives, some of them experience the love and life of the Holy Spirit.

For others in this group, the *Charismatic* experience may only be a new devotion to their religion, without a personal relationship with Jesus Christ. These may, or may not emphasize ecstatic utterances.

O   **Catholic Charismatics**

Catholic Charismatics are from the Catholic Church. They usually undergo a renewal in their faith and commitment to their church through contact with a *Charismatic* group.

Some undergo true born again conversion while others become more devout religious practitioners. These may or may not emphasize ecstatic utterances.

Brief Historical Overview

The Pentecostal Movement is a relatively new movement in Church History. Church historians place its birth near the beginning of the twentieth century.

Church historian, Bill Austin, in his, *Topical History of Christianity*, traces the birth of the *Pentecostal Movement* to April 1906, in Los Angeles, during the *Azusa Street Revival*. At those meeting it was officially reported, for the first time, that people *spoke in tongues*. They claimed this *speaking in tongues,* was a revival of what the early church did on that first day of *Pentecost*, following Christ's resurrection.

Austin states many *Pentecostal* denominations try to trace their origins to 1886, during the *Latter Rain Revival* in the Great Smoky Mountains.

Frank S. Mead, church historian, and author of, *Handbook of Denominations in the United States*, traces the *Pentecostal Movement* back to August 18, 1886, in Monroe County, Tennessee, when the *Latter Rain Revival*, or *Appalachian Holiness Revival*, as it is known, began.

It was on that date, a Baptist minister by the name of Richard G. Spurling formed *The Christian Union*. It is said Spurling claimed to have been, *led by the Bible to stem the tide of the churches' spiritual indifference, formality and accommodation to modern culture.*

The Christian Union, which Spurling organized, later became known as *The Church of God* (Cleveland, Tennessee). That body of believers had a strong emphasis on salvation by faith and on personal holiness wrought in one's life by a subsequent act of the Holy Spirit. Theologians refer to that teaching as *Entire Sanctification. Church of God* leaders, claim

Spurling taught *Entire Sanctification* was evidenced by the practice of, *speaking in tongues* (ecstatic utterances).

Grant Wacker, in *Eerdmans's Handbook to Christianity in America*, traces the beginning of the *Pentecostal Movement* to the preaching and writings of Charles Fox Parham, an itinerant faith healer, and to a revival meeting he led in Topeka, Kansas in 1901. At that meeting, people are reported to have *spoken in tongues* (ecstatic utterances).

Parham insisted all Christians should seek the *Baptism of the Holy Spirit*, which he taught is accompanied by *speaking in tongues*.

As this movement spread, many groups adopted what Parham referred to as, the *Pentecostal experience of speaking in tongues*. In the years that followed, the word *Pentecostal*, was attached to this movement.

After the beginning of the twentieth century, a number of denominations formed, which identified themselves as *Pentecostal*. One of the largest *Pentecostal* bodies, *The Assemblies of God*, was organized in Hot Springs, Arkansas in 1914.

The Assemblies of God teach a *Baptism of the Holy Spirit*, as something which occurs after salvation, and which gives believers the *fullness of the Holy Spirit*. This baptism is evidenced by *speaking in tongues* (ecstatic utterances).

The Charismatic Movement started a number of years after the *Pentecostal Movement*. Some claim the *Charismatic Movement* was given birth by the *Pentecostal Movement*, others claim it sprung up independently.

The Charismatic Movement surfaced in the 1960's during what some call, the *Anti-War Hippie Era*. In its infancy, theologians and observers called the *Charismatic Movement*, *The Neo-Pentecostal Movement*. It spread rapidly when articles about it appeared in *Time* and *Newsweek* magazines.

Many young people from main-line churches were disillusioned by what they saw as a lack of love and lack of power in their churches. A Christian counter-culture, referred to as the *Jesus People*, developed. *Jesus People* held rallies and concerts across the country. In many ways, their clothing and music resembled the hippie counter-culture of the 1960's. *Jesus People* rallies and concerts gave birth to numerous Bible studies and coffeehouse ministries. As the movement grew, it infiltrated many churches and spread from young people to those in every age group.

The love of God and the *person* and *power* of the Holy Spirit were the main topics emphasized by the *Jesus People*. They adopted many *Pentecostal* tendencies, such as enthusiastic worship and raising hands. That drew in a number of *Pentecostal* sympathizers who helped influence the theology of the movement. Many people in the movement continued to maintain ties with the churches they came from. Some left their churches and formed non-denominational congregations.

This movement was first called the *Neo-Pentecostal (New Pentecostal) Movement* because of its *Pentecostal* tendencies. Unlike *Old Pentecostalism*, it did not teach all believers must speak in ecstatic utterances; hence, it was a *New Pentecostalism*. A number of the *Neo-Pentecostal* groups do not practice *speaking in tongues.*

I was part of the *Jesus People* Movement. It was not until I was involved in this movement for a few years that I first heard someone speak in tongues (*ecstatic utterances*).

As the *Neo-Pentecostal* movement began to grow, it spread rapidly. Those who wanted to give it a separate identity from *Pentecostalism* gave it a new name. The name, *the Charismatic Movement*, was adopted. The term *Charismatic*, came from the Greek Word for *Spiritual Gifts*, **charismaton**, which is found in 1 Corinthians 12:4.

The choice of the word *Charismatic* to identify *Neo-Pentecostalism* has caused a lot of confusion. Today, when someone mentions *Spiritual Gifts* most people immediately think of the *Charismatic Movement* and its definitions. A better name for the movement would have been the *Pneumatic Movement*, based on the Greek word, **pneumatikon**, which is found in 1 Corinthians 12:1, which means, *things pertaining to the Holy Spirit.*

As the *Charismatic Movement* grew, it shed the counter-culture image of the *Jesus People*. Its growth exploded with the formation of the *Full Gospel Business Men's Fellowship* and cassette tape ministries, which were promoted by *Charismatic* teachers like Rev. Dennis Bennett and Rev. Everett *Terry* Fullam, both Episcopal Charismatic priests. These had a powerful effect, which helped spread the *Charismatic Movement*. My mother ran the international tape ministry for Terry Fulham.

Old-time *Pentecostal* preachers like Oral Roberts, Rex Humbard and Jimmy Swaggart, soon aligned themselves with the *Pentecostal* tendencies within the *Charismatic Movement*. Soon this *New Pentecostalism* dominated the airwaves on Christian Radio and Television.

The birth of Pat Robertson's *Christian Broadcasting Network* and Jim Bakker's *P.T.L. Club*, helped spread the *Charismatic* message internationally, via television.

The Doctrine of Charismatics & Pentecostals

It is important to understand it is *experience*, not necessarily *doctrine*, which is the unifying force in the *Charismatic Movement*. Doctrinal differences among *Charismatics* and *Pentecostals* can be vast. Many are truly born again Christians some are not. Many *Charismatics* hold to most of the fundamental doctrines while some question such foundational truths as inspiration and redemption.

There are three general areas of consent among *Pentecostals* and *Charismatics*:

1.   The Baptism of the Spirit

Each group believes in a subsequent work of grace, after salvation, whereby one receives the *fullness of the Holy Spirit*. They refer to this as the *Baptism of (or in) the Spirit*.

This is where the term, *Full Gospel,* comes in. Those who have the subsequent work of the Holy Spirit, as taught by the *Pentecostals* and *Charismatics*, are said to have the Full Gospel.

Those who do not have this work do not have the Full Gospel. Both groups place a strong emphasis on seeking this *Baptism of the Spirit*.

Some people in these movements *grieve* the Holy Spirit by claiming believers outside their movement do not have the *fullness* or *power* of the Holy Spirit.

2.   A Universal, Invisible Church

Most of these groups believe all believers, in a broad sense, are joint members of a mystical Body of Christ regardless of denomination. There is a measure of truth in this, in that, all born again believers are members of the *Family of God* (Ephesians 2:18-19), and one day will be gathered together as one glorious church (Ephesians 4:27).

Pentecostals and *Charismatics* apply the word, *church*, in almost all of its uses, to refer to the *Universal Family of God*. They tend to blur the distinction between *the Family of God* and *the Local Church*. They believe God's plan for the ages is accomplished when the members of the *Universal Church* worship together, regardless of location or organization. This lends itself strongly to ecumenical activity, which often overlooks important doctrinal distinctions and the Biblical emphasis on the Local Church in God's plan. It also tends to disregard the scriptural call to keep separate from apostates and false teachers (2 Corinthians 6:14-18).

One danger is those who claim the *Pentecostal* or *Charismatic* experience are often welcomed in some of those churches, without being examined doctrinally. This led to many false teachers and charlatans infiltrating and misleading well-meaning groups of believers in those movements, thus giving them a bad name.

It is also important to remember a number of false religious groups and cults, such as *The Church of Jesus Christ of Latter Day Saints* (*Mormons*), claim a *Charismatic* type experience and use similar terminology.

3.   Extra-Biblical Revelation

Each of these groups generally believe God directs people

today as He did the prophets in the Old Testament. They believe this is done either through prophesy, visions or what they call *Tongues* (*ecstatic utterances*). These manifestations are believed to carry God's authority, often with as much authority as the written Word of God.

This belief is one that can cause a very shaky foundation for a *Pentecostal* and *Charismatic*. Even though they often love and respect the Word of God, the absolute standard of God's complete revelation to man, which is found only in the Bible, is supplanted and a shaky subjective foundation is left in its place. Many times, there is not an objective standard by which the additional revelation can be judged. In fact, if you question it, you are often judged.

This belief can open people up to various questionable teachings, which claim revelation from God. Such extra-Biblical revelation is an important part of *Mormonism* and other cults.

Tongues

One practice almost universally followed by *Pentecostals*, and many *Charismatics*, is called *Speaking in Tongues*. *Pentecostals* see this as **the evidence** one has received the *Baptism of the Holy Spirit*. *Charismatics* see *Speaking in Tongues* as **only one of the possible evidences** of the *Baptism of the Holy Spirit*. Most people in both groups refer to those tongues as a *Spiritual Gift*.

As we have seen in this book, *Tongues* is not listed in Scripture as one of the *Spiritual Gifts*. *Tongues* is found in the Bible in the list of *Ministries* and in the list of *Results* granted sovereignly by God.

The Two Basic Views As To What Tongues Are:

1.   The Ecstatic View

This view teaches *Speaking in Tongues* is the ability to speak in non-earthly, heavenly languages. These languages will often sound unintelligible to the normal listener. An interpreter is required for others to understand what is said.

The ecstatic view is based partially on 1 Corinthians 13:1, where it speaks of *tongues of men and of angels*. Many who hold this view claim they are speaking in the tongues of angels.

> Though I speak with the tongues of men and of angels, and have not charity, I am become as a sounding brass, or a tinkling cymbal.
>
> 1 Corinthians 13:1

Those who oppose this view, argue that every time, without exception, when angels are mentioned as speaking, in the Bible, they spoke in known human languages. Two examples of this are: when the angels came to Lot in Sodom (Genesis 19) and when they appeared to the shepherds to announce the birth of Christ (Luke 2). In each of these instances, the angels spoke in the language of the people they were addressing. There is not any instance in the Bible where angels speak in languages other than those understandable to those they address.

Those who do not accept the ecstatic utterance view, believe the context of 1 Corinthians 13:1, is referring to the supremacy of love, over anything, even over the eloquent concise words of men or angels. In Scripture, angels usually use few words but get their point across clearly.

Those who hold to the ecstatic view usually teach tongues are a *Spiritual Gift* available to all, or to most believers who will ask for it. They often view this as a special heavenly language to be used in prayer. Many use 1 Corinthians 14:2, as their proof text.

> He that speaketh in an unknown tongue speaketh not unto men, but unto God: for no man understandeth him; howbeit in the spirit he speaketh mysteries.
>
> 1 Corinthians 14:2

Proponents of the ecstatic utterance view, point out the Apostle Paul, spoke in tongues (1 Corinthians 14:18). It is true Paul spoke in tongues. In fact, he spoke in many tongues. Scholars claim he spoke Hebrew, Greek, Aramaic and Latin. Paul probably prayed in these languages, depending on whom he was with. Some of his prayers may have sounded like ecstatic utterances to those who did not understand those other languages if he prayed in using them.

Paul said it is possible to pray in a language we do not understand (1 Corinthians 14:14). I saw this as I was growing up. My mother's parents were Norwegian, so we would often pray a prayer in Norwegian before our meals. I could pronounce it and even enjoyed saying it. As Paul said, my spirit profited (*I felt good about what I did*), but my mind did not know what it meant.

Something similar happened in the homes of a number of my friends in the Jewish neighborhood where I grew up. As part of their religious training, some of them memorized Hebrew prayers. They even taught me some. Neither they, nor I, knew what they meant at that time. All they knew was it meant something good. Though the mind did not profit, it made their spirits feel good. Paul said he preferred to pray in languages he understood, so both his spirit and his mind would benefit (1 Corinthians 14:15-19).

Those who oppose the ecstatic utterance view of tongues, teach 1 Corinthians 14, refers to a person from another culture who speaks another language, or to one who prays or preaches in a known earthly language, which no one in the group they are with understands. They may feel good about it, and God will understand them, but no one else present will be able to figure it out, unless they have an interpreter. If they do have an interpreter, all will be able to profit from it. If an unbeliever walks in from that other language group, and hears their own language, it could be a clear sign to the unbeliever God loves them. That interpretation fits well in a cultural melting pot and trade center like Corinth and in many areas of the world today. It emphasizes the importance of linguistic *ministries* in the church.

As far as we can tell, and *Pentecostal* historians agree, there are no instances of ecstatic utterances happening among believers before 1886. If ecstatic utterances are the correct interpretation, opponents claim godly men and women would have practiced this prior to that date and left some kind of record behind.

In my forty plus years of ministry around the world, meeting thousands of Believers, I never met anyone who studied the Word of God by themselves, without outside influence, and arrived at the conclusion believers were to speak in ecstatic utterances. The only way any believer I ever met came to accept the teaching of ecstatic utterance was if others introduced that concept to them. If it were Biblical, it would seem the Holy Spirit could illuminate people to understand this truth directly from the Scriptures.

Some ask, what is happening in the lives of those believers who pray in ecstatic utterances, if that is not Biblical tongues? That is a very good question. As I stated before, new believers must be taught by someone else the concept of ecstatic utterances is something they must practice. When they see other believers, who they admire and respect, practice ecstatic utterances and are taught they must do the same to be a good Christian, many of them will find a way to do it.

I have personally known *Pentecostal* teachers who take new believers aside and teach them how to *speak in tongues*. Often they tell their pupils to speak without thinking, to relax and let the sounds come forth. No such instruction occurred, nor is taught in the Bible.

As with any spiritual practice, some who practice ecstatic utterances are faking it. Many have told me that was the case in their lives. They know what they are doing is not from the Holy Spirit, but they do it anyway. Some do it because they are told that is what a spiritual believer is supposed to do, so they do it to be accepted or to impress others. Some do it as a matter of pride or to attain spiritual status in a group.

With some, what occurs as they seek to *speak in tongues* is an emotional experience. It is very hard to reason with someone who has an emotional experience. People who get involved in something emotionally often lose their objectivity.

Some opponents go too far and say ecstatic utterances are demonic. There are *some* cases where that is true. I have seen sincere people seeking the ability to pray in ecstatic utterances open themselves up to demonic influences, from which they later needed deliverance. Though that is the case with some who *speak in tongues,* I do not believe that is the case with most people who *speak in tongues.*

Those who hold to the ecstatic utterance interpretation of tongues often misunderstand the distinctions and purpose of the *Three-Fold Work of the Holy Spirit* in the life of the Believer. They are looking for a *filling* to give them a closer deeper personal relationship with God, instead of looking for a *filling* to help them relate effectively with others or to get Holy Spirit *power* for service. That closer, deeper relationship with the Lord is not some special ecstatic experience. It is something available to all believers as part of the *Indwelling,* and comes in response to obedience and a personal daily walk with the Lord.

2. The Human Language View

This view teaches Biblical tongues are the ability to speak in human languages. This is based on the Greek word for tongues, **glossa**, which is translated in all other literature and in other places in the Bible as *languages.*

> Wherefore let him that speaketh in an unknown tongue pray that he may interpret.
>
> 1 Corinthians 14:13

The word *interpret,* (1 Corinthians 14:13), is the translation of the Greek word, **dihermeneuo**, which means *to translate.* This word is used in all other Greek literature for translating one known human language to another.

In summary, this verse says, if you speak another language others do not understand, you should pray God will help you translate your words into the language of the people you are with, so everyone can understand you.

> And they were all filled with the Holy Ghost, and began to speak with other tongues, as the Spirit gave them utterance. And there were dwelling at Jerusalem Jews, devout men, out of every nation under heaven. Now when this was noised abroad, the multitude came together, and were confounded, because every man heard them speak in his own language.
>
> Acts 2:4-6

The Human Language view contends at Pentecost (Acts 2), when the believers were *filled* with *the power of the Holy Spirit*, they spoke in known human languages, not ecstatic utterances. *Pentecostals* challenge this by claiming the believers *spoke* in ecstatic utterances but the people *heard* what was said in their own language.

Besides claiming consistency with the proper rules of Biblical Hermeneutics, those who hold the Human Language view express concern because the ecstatic language view is the view liberals, who reject the Bible, agree with. Buddhists, Hindus, Mormons and Occult groups all endorse and practice ecstatic utterances.

Among those who hold to the **Unlearned Human Languages** viewpoint on Tongues there are two distinct groups:

○ **Tongues Were a Sign Gift, Which Ceased.**

These view the ability to speak an unlearned human language as a *Sign Gift*, given by God to authenticate the message of the Gospel, until the written word could be circulated (1 Corinthians 13:8). They teach, once the written Word of God was complete and authenticated, tongues ceased. As we have seen from Scripture, tongues is not identified as a *Spiritual Gift*.

○ **Tongues are a Linguistic Ministry.**

These view tongues, not as a *Gift* but as a linguistic ministry or sovereignly given *Result*. They view the event on the day of Pentecost as a supernatural extension of this ministry. They do not rule out the possibility, and need, of such a supernatural act of God.

They believe tongues are usually a linguistic ministry. The majority of people who have this ministry, and want to function more effectively, must learn it through study and discipleship. That is the same way people in other *ministries* learn how to develop skills, seeking the help of the Holy Spirit to be more effective.

Conclusion

Whether or not you agree with the doctrine of the *Pentecostals* and *Charismatics*, they breathed a breath of new life into Christianity, when it seemed, in many circles, to have stagnated. They also caused people to take a much-needed closer look at the Holy Spirit.

It is important to look carefully at the Bible to see what it says about the Holy Spirit and about the role; He wants to play in our lives. Do not blindly accept what other people say. Study the Word of God and let it be your final guide for what you believe and for what you do.

CHAPTER FIFTEEN
QUESTIONS

Verse to Memorize: I Thessalonians 5:19

15.1   What is a *Pentecostal*?

15.2   What are the three different types of *Charismatics*?

15.3   What are the three general areas of consent among *Pentecostals* and *Charismatics*?

15.4   What are the two major views on Tongues?

15.5   What are the two different views held by those who believe Tongues are a Human Language?

QUESTIONS FOR ADDITIONAL THOUGHT

15.6   What is the unifying force among *Charismatics* and what are some of the implications of this?

15.7   What is the *Pentecostal* and *Charismatic* viewpoint on Revelation and Inspiration? Why does this create a shaky foundation?

15.8   After completing this study, which viewpoint, regarding tongues, makes the most sense to you and why?

CLOSING THOUGHTS

God told us He does not want us to be ignorant regarding the Holy Spirit. After reading this book, I pray you have a better understanding of who the Holy Spirit is and what He does.

You may not agree with everything presented in this book, but if you are a believer, would you do the following?

- ○ Thank God for Giving You the Holy Spirit of God.
- ○ Allow the Holy Spirit to Work in Your Life.
- ○ Ask God to *Fill* You with the Holy Spirit for Your Daily Relationships.
- ○ Understand You Have a *Spiritual Gift*, Which Differs from What Some Other People Have. Accept Your Unique Perspective on Life, as Well as Others, and Learn How to Work Together for God's Glory.
- ○ Find the *Place of Ministry* God Has for You.
- ○ Ask God to *Empower* You as You Serve Him.
- ○ Share His Love and Light with Others.

> For this cause I bow my knees unto the Father of our Lord Jesus Christ, of whom the whole family in heaven and earth is named, that He would grant you, according to the riches of His glory, to be strengthened with might by His Spirit in the inner man; that Christ may dwell in your hearts by faith; that ye, being rooted and grounded in love, may be able to comprehend with all the saints what is the breadth, and length, and depth and height; and to know the love of Christ, which passeth knowledge, that ye might be filled with all the fullness of God. Now unto Him that is able to do exceeding abundantly above all that we ask or think, according to the power that worketh in us, unto Him be glory in the church by Christ Jesus throughout all ages, world without end. Amen.
>
> Ephesians 3:14-21

Dr. Larry A. Maxwell

APPENDIX

Laying on Hands

Neglect not the gift that is in thee, which was given thee by prophesy, with the laying on of the hands of the presbytery.   1 Timothy 4:14

In Chapter 13 of this book, the teaching is presented that each believer has only one *Spiritual Gift*. One verse some Bible scholars use to prove we each have only one *Spiritual Gift* is 1 Timothy 4:14. I was one of those who used that verse as one of my proof texts for a number of years. One day, I sat down and critically challenged everything I was teaching about the *Gifts*. I arrived at a different conclusion regarding this passage.

In 1 Timothy 4:14, Paul told Timothy he had a *gift*, which he got because of the *laying on of the hands* of the presbytery. Some avoid this verse because of its reference to *Laying on Hands*. Laying hands on others has become an area of controversy many would like to avoid. This passage, and the practice of *Laying on Hands*, cannot be ignored. This bears some careful investigation.

There are at least three different types of *Laying on Hands* referred to in the New Testament. Each one has a distinct purpose and meaning (Hebrews 6:2).

1.   Laying on Hands to Heal The Sick.

The New Testament Church laid hands on those who were sick, to seek their healing, just as Jesus did (Mark 16:18). This practice is listed in the closing words of the Gospel of Mark as one of the *results*, which would happen after Christ ascended.

Some claim this was fulfilled in the Book of Acts, and is not for today. Peter, John and Paul all laid hands on people and saw them healed. It is interesting to note these three leaders of the church are the only ones specifically recorded in the Bible to have laid hands on people and seen them healed.

None of the epistles specifically instructs us to lay hands on others to heal them.

Some claim laying hands on others to heal them is a practice for the church today. Perhaps the passage in James 5:13-16 could be interpreted to mean laying hands on others for healing, though it does not say to *lay hands* on someone. This action, in this passage, is a function for the leaders in the church.

> Is any among you afflicted? Let him pray. Is any merry? Let him sing psalms. Is any sick among you? Let him call for the elders of the church; and let them pray over him, anointing him with oil in the name of the Lord: and the prayer of faith shall save the sick, and the Lord shall raise him up; and if he have committed sins, they shall be forgiven him. Confess your faults one to another, and pray for one another, that ye may be healed. The effectual fervent prayer of a righteous man availeth much.　　　　　　　　　　James 5:13-16

Even though the Scriptures do not specifically exhort all believers to lay hands on one another for healing, it certainly does exhort us all to *pray for one another*. Though you may not be able to claim specific authority from God to lay hands on others to heal them, there is nothing wrong with laying hands on someone else and submissively praying for God to heal them, then leaving the results up to God.

2.　　Laying on Hands to Convey the Power of the Holy Spirit.

Though Jesus often laid hands on people to heal them, it is interesting to note the Bible never records an instance where Jesus laid his hands on anyone to give them the Holy Spirit.

There are three unique instances in the New Testament where believers had the *Indwelling of the Holy Spirit* but did not receive the *Empowering of the Holy Spirit* until church leaders laid hands on them.

○　　In Acts 8:14-17, Peter and John went to Samaria to confirm the preaching of Philip. Prior to that, God used Philip to see many Samaritans saved and baptized (Acts 7:4-13).

> Now when the apostles which were at Jerusalem heard that Samaria had received the word of God, they sent

> unto them Peter and John: who, when they prayed for
> them, that they might receive the Holy Ghost: (For as
> yet He was fallen **upon** none of them: only they were
> baptized in the name of the Lord Jesus). Then laid they
> their hands on them, and they received the Holy Ghost.
>
> Acts 8:14-17

Verse 15, says though the Samaritan believers were saved, they had not received the Holy Spirit. Some people misunderstood that to mean they did not receive the *Indwelling of the Holy Spirit*. God foresaw the possibility of confusion, so in verse 16, He explained what they lacked was the Holy Spirit coming **upon** them. That is the term for the *Empowering of the Holy Spirit*, not the *Indwelling*.

The Bible is very clear, ever since Christ was glorified, all believers receive the Holy Spirit the moment they are saved (John 7:38-39; Acts 20:22). [Refer also to the Chapter Eight, *The Holy Spirit and the Saved, The Indwelling*, and to Chapter Ten, *The Holy Spirit and the Saved, the Empowering*].

Peter and John laid hands on the believers in Samaria and they received the *Empowering* of the Holy Spirit. They already had the *Indwelling*, no one but God can give that to anyone. They were used, in this special situation, to give them the *Empowering*. This *Empowering* is a special benefit God sovereignly gives us when we serve Him.

The Jews and Samaritans, as two different ethnic groups, had a long hatred and mistrust towards one another. Perhaps that is why God had Peter and John, two saved Jewish leaders in the church, go to Samaria to confer on those believers one of the benefits of serving the Lord. This showed both groups, the wall was broken down and they were serving the same God, through the same Holy Spirit.

O   The Second Incident where people received the *Empowering* of the Holy Spirit with hands laid on them is recorded in Acts 9:17, after Paul was saved on his way to persecute the Christians in Damascus.

> And Ananias went his way, and entered into the house;
> and putting his hands on him said, Brother Saul, the Lord,
> even Jesus, that appeared unto thee in the way as thou

camest, hath sent me, that thou mightest receive thy sight and be filled with the Holy Ghost.

Acts 9:17

The same thing that happened to the believers in Samaria happened to Paul. This time, Ananias, one of the leaders of the church, which Paul was coming to persecute, was sent by God to help disciple Paul. Ananias laid hands on him and Paul was *Filled with the Holy Spirit.*

This was a *filling with the power of the Holy Spirit* for the special ministry the Lord had for Paul. Paul was to become the Apostle to the Gentiles (Acts 9:15-16).

○   The Third Incident is found in Acts 19:1-7. Paul met some disciples at Ephesus, who were saved, but had not followed the Lord in Believer's Baptism.

And it came to pass, that, while Apollos was at Corinth, Paul having passed through the upper coasts came to Ephesus: and finding certain disciples, he said unto them, Have ye received the Holy Ghost since ye believed? And they said unto him, We have not so much as heard whether there be any Holy Ghost: And he said unto them, Unto what then were ye baptized? And they said, Unto John's baptism. Then said Paul, John verily baptized with the baptism of repentance, saying unto the people, that they should believe on Him which should come after him, that is, on Christ Jesus. When they heard this, they were baptized in the name of the Lord Jesus. And when Paul had laid hands on them, the Holy Ghost came **on** them; and they spake in tongues and prophesied. And all the men were about twelve.

Acts 19:1-6

These believers were familiar with John the Baptist but not with the Holy Spirit. This shows it is possible to have the Holy Spirit and not know it. After they followed the Lord in Believer's Baptism, Paul laid hands on them and the Holy Spirit came *on them.*

Notice the words *on them*, were used. Those are the words used to describe the *Empowering of the Holy Spirit* for service, not the *Indwelling of the Holy Spirit*. Because of receiving the

Empowering of the Holy Spirit, those believers, in that multi-cultural area, spoke in other languages (*tongues*) and proclaimed God's Word to others (*prophesied*).

Notice how service followed the *Empowering*. Perhaps the Lord held back the *Empowering of the Holy Spirit* from these believers, till Paul came, to show people a *preparatory baptism* like John's, or that followed by many denominations today, is not enough. Those who are saved are to be baptized after they are saved, regardless of how many times they have been baptized before, and then they are to serve the Lord in the *power* of the Holy Spirit.

Jesus did not tell his disciples to lay hands on others so they could receive the *power* of the Holy Spirit. This Laying on Hands to convey the *power* of the Holy Spirit did not happen on the Day of Pentecost, when the first *Empowering* took place, nor did it take place at any other time in the New Testament, except in the above three unique recorded instances. Each instance was done to teach us something special about serving the Lord.

Laying on Hands on others is not mentioned as a normal part of any ministry in the Bible. There are not any passages of Scripture, which tell us we are to lay hands on others to impart the *power* of the Holy Spirit to them. God will sovereignly give His *Empowering* to those who seek it. It appears this aspect of Laying Hands on Others is not a practice to be followed by the Church today.

3. Laying On Hands to Ordain for Ministry

In the Bible, we also find the practice of laying hands on someone to ordain them for ministry. It is this Laying on Hands, which we refer to today as *ordination*. That is what Paul referred to in 1 Timothy 4:14.

Before ordaining someone, the leaders in a church prayed and confirmed the fact God prepared an individual for a particular ministry. This *ordination* was either for a ministry *to* the churches (Ephesians 4:11-12) or for the office of a Deacon (Acts 6:1-7). After prayerfully seeking God's will, the Church leaders laid their hands on the individual, *confirming their endorsement* of the individual and that person's ministry. All *ministries* therefore derived their authority from a Local Church.

This practice of *Laying on Hands* to *ordain* someone for ministry has its roots in the Old Testament priesthood. The Lord told Moses to set the Levites apart for service. The Levites were then brought to the people, who were to lay their hands on them. This symbolized the *endorsement* of the individuals and the conferring of authority on them to minister on behalf of the people (Numbers 8:10-11).

> And thou shalt bring the Levites before the LORD: and the children of Israel shall put their hands upon the Levites: and Aaron shall offer the Levites before the LORD for an offering of the children of Israel, that they may execute the service of the LORD.
>
> Numbers 8:10-11

In another Old Testament passage, we find Moses laying his hands on Joshua, to designate him as his successor to lead the Children of Israel into the Promised Land (Deuteronomy 34:9).

> And Joshua the son of Nun was full of the spirit of wisdom; for Moses had laid his hands upon him: and the children of Israel hearkened unto him, and he did as the LORD commanded Moses.   Deuteronomy 34:9

In Mark 3:14, it says Jesus *ordained* the twelve. It is possible to imply from this passage, and about what we see in relationship to ordination for ministry in other passages, Jesus may have laid hands on the twelve.

This practice of Laying on Hands by the leaders in a church (*ordination*) is found in the following passages:

○   **Acts 6:1-7** - The Twelve Apostles told the Church at Jerusalem to choose seven godly men to handle the business of the Church. Then the apostles ordained those men.

> And the saying pleased the whole multitude: and they chose Stephen, a man full of faith and the Holy Ghost, and Philip, and Prochorus, and Nicanor, and Timon, and Parmenas, and Nicholas a proselyte of Antioch: whom they set before the apostles: and when they had prayed,

> they laid hands on them. And the Word of God increased;
> and the number of the disciples multiplied in Jerusalem
> greatly; and a great company of the priests were obedient
> to the faith.
>
> Acts 6:5-7

○ **Acts 13:1-3** - The Lord told certain elders in the church at Antioch to ordain Paul and Barnabas for missionary work.

> As they ministered to the Lord, and fasted, the Holy
> Ghost said, Separate me Barnabas and Saul for the work
> whereunto I have called them. And when they had fasted
> and prayed, and laid their hands on them, they sent them
> away.
>
> Acts 13:2-3

○ **Acts 14:23** - Paul ordained leaders for the various churches. It does not specifically say he laid hands on them but it is probable he did.

> And when they had ordained them elders in every
> church, and had prayed with fasting, they commended
> them to the Lord, on whom they believed.
>
> Acts 14:23

○ **1 Timothy 4:14; 2 Timothy 1:6** - Timothy was ordained by Paul and other Church leaders.

> Neglect not the gift that is in thee, which was given thee
> by prophesy, with the laying on of the hands of the
> presbytery.
>
> 1 Timothy 4:14

○ **1 Timothy 5:22** - Paul cautioned Timothy to be careful about who he ordained.

> Lay hands suddenly on no man...   1 Timothy 5:22

In 1 Timothy 4:14, Paul exhorted Timothy to, *stir up the gift that is in thee*. Paul referred to this *gift* in the singular sense. Some have said Paul was referring to Timothy's *Spiritual Gift*. The problem with that interpretation is, Paul says the *gift* was, *given thee by prophesy* (the *Gift*, or *Ministry*, of preaching or proclaiming God's Word)*, with the laying on of the hands of the presbytery* (ordination by leaders in the church). As we have seen in this study, the Scriptures teach us the Lord gives our

241

Spiritual Gift to us, man does not. That being the case, *the gift* Paul is referring to must be some *gift* other than Timothy's *Spiritual Gift.*

Perhaps Paul was reminding Timothy the *Ministry*, which had become such an intrinsic part of his life, was not something he earned, but a *gift* which was entrusted to him by the church. It was Timothy's responsibility to stir up that *gift* and use it to serve the Lord through His church.

ABOUT THE AUTHOR

Dr. Larry A. Maxwell attended Practical Bible Training School *(now Davis College)* in Johnson City, New York, then Lynchburg Baptist College in Lynchburg, Virginia *(which changed its name to Liberty Baptist College and is now called Liberty University)*. He majored in Pastoral Ministry, Youth Ministry and Biblical Studies. He later earned both a Maters and Doctors degree in Biblical Studies from the India Theological Seminary in Brahmavar, India.

He was ordained to the Gospel Ministry in 1976, by his pastor, Dr. Jerry Falwell and *Thomas Road Baptist Church* in Lynchburg, Virginia, where he was a member.

He served as a Church Planter, Youth Pastor and Pastor. For many years he was listed as an Associate Evangelist, with *The Sword of the Lord.*

Dr. Maxwell founded *Challenge International* in 1981, to help *Challenge Others to Greater Service for Christ.* With *Challenge International* he serves as an advisor to pastors, church boards and other organizations.

He teaches on both the undergraduate and graduate level. He served as academic dean of the *Colonial Hills Baptist College* and of *The India Theological Seminary International Extension.*

He is a popular conference speaker and award-winning author.

Some of the books he authored include:

- How to Find the Right Pastor
- Gaining Personal Financial Freedom, through the Biblical Principles of Finances
- Gaining Financial Freedom Budget Workbook
- More Than 500 Proven Ways to Reduce Expenses
- Becoming a Dynamic Youth Leader
- 175 Ways to Fund Your Youth Ministry
- You Can Start a Local Church Bible Institute
- The Round Up – Vacation Bible School Manual

To contact Dr. Larry A. Maxwell with questions, or to schedule him for a conference, consultation or to speak, go to his website: LarryMaxwell.com

Selected Bibliography

These are listed for Reference purposes ONLY.
This is NOT an Endorsement of the Content of These Books.

Brown, Colin, editor   The New International Dictionary of New Testament Theology, Grand Rapids: Regency Reference Library, Zondervan, *Copyright 1967.*

Cambron, Mark G.   Bible Doctrines, Beliefs That Matter, Grand Rapids: Zondervan Publishing House, *Copyright 1954.*

Coy, Larry   Design for Successful Living, Lynchburg: Victorious Ventures, *Copyright 1975.*

Geisler & Nix   General Introduction to the Bible, Chicago: Moody Press, *Copyright 1968*

Hendriksen, William   New Testament Commentary, The Gospel of John, Grand Rapids: Baker Book House, *Copyright 1953.*

Henry, Matthew   Matthew Henry's Commentary, Grand Rapids: Zondervan Publishing House, *Copyright 1960.*

Flynn, Leslie B.   19 Gifts of the Spirit,   Wheaton: Victor Books, *Copyright 1974.*

Legters, L.L.   The Simplicity of the Spirit-Filled Life, Farmingdale: Christian Witness Products, *Copyright 1930,52,68.*

Mead, Frank S.   Handbook of Denominations In the United States Nashville: Abingdon Press, *Copyright 1951, 1985.*

Rice, John R.   The Charismatic Movement, Murfreesboro: Sword of the Lord Publishers, *Copyright 1976.*

Rice, John R.   The Power of Pentecost, Murfreesboro: Sword of the Lord Publishers, *Copyright 1949.*

Sanders, J. Oswald   The Holy Spirit and His Gifts, Grand Rapids: Zondervan Publishing House, *Copyright 1940.*

Strauss, Lehman The Third Person, Neptune: Loizeau Brothers, *Copyright 1954.*

Torrey, R.A. How to Succeed in the Christian Life, Chicago: Moody Press, *No Copyright.*

Walvoord, John F. The Holy Spirit, Grand Rapids: Zondervan Publishing House, *Copyright 1954,58.*

Walvoord, John F. & Zuck, Roy B., editors The Bible Knowledge Commentary, Wheaton: Victor Books, *Copyright 1983.*

Wemp, C. Sumner How On Earth Can I Be Spiritual? Nashville: Thomas Nelson Inc., Publishers, *Copyright 1978.*

Willmington, Harold L. Willmington's Guide to the Bible, Wheaton: Tyndale House Publishers, *Copyright 1981.*

Woods, Gary C. Guide to Theologians, San Diego: Excelsior Press, *Copyright 2010.*

Subject Index

Dr. Larry A. Maxwell

Dr. Larry A. Maxwell

148, 163, 165, 204-205, 209, 226-227, 235, 237-239, 241-242
Pastor ... 120, 206-207-208
Pasture ... 207
Pentecost ... 141-143, 145, 220, 229-230, 239
Pentecostal ... 12, 20-22, 140, 142, 259-162, 164, 215, 217-231
Persevere ... 101-103, 105, 107
Personal Benefits ... 129
Personality Type ... 181
Personhood ... 19-20, 28, 30, 35, 40-41, 45, 47, 113
Perspective ... 49, 125, 165, 175, 178-179, 181, 184, 192, 195-199, 201-202, 210, 233
Peter ... 71, 204, 235
Platform ... 133, 202
Pneumatic Movement ... 222
Pneumatology ... 15-16, 18
Potential ... 49, 125, 165, 175, 177, 179, 181, 196-197, 199, 201
Power ... 13, 18, 31-32, 42, 45-46, 56-61, 70-71, 74, 178-79, 82-86, 111-114, 119-120, 125, 129, 131, 136, 139-149, 151, 153-157, 162-163, 168-174, 212, 221-222, 224, 229, 233, 236-239
Practical Bible ... 12
Prayer ... 28, 41, 43, 123, 128-130, 202-203, 226-227, 239
Preservation ... 73
Presuppositions ... 23, 159, 175-176
Professional Ministry ... 203-210
Promise ... 37, 57, 145
Prophesy ... 159, 161-162, 171, 176, 180, 187-189, 191, 224, 241
Prophet ... 69-71, 147, 176, 187-191, 194-195, 198, 202, 205-206, 211, 215, 224
Propitiation ... 93

Protestant Reformation ... 19, 101
Provision ... 49, 99, 122, 124, 165
Quenching ... 151, 153-156
Rapture ... 92
Received Greek ... 13
Regeneration ... 43, 99-100, 197
Relationship ... 11, 30, 34, 39, 46, 53, 77-79, 95, 99, 112-113, 125, 127-136, 139-140, 145, 149, 154, 191, 219, 229, 233
Remonstrance ... 101
Renew ... 48, 219
Reprove ... 46, 93, 102, 106, 121
Resist ... 34, 102-104
Restrain ... 47, 56, 89, 91-92
Results ... 149,159, 165, 167-173, 175-176, 184, 187, 201, 215, 225, 230
Resurrection ... 43, 53-54, 77, 94, 99, 114, 141, 145, 148, 204, 218, 220
Revelation ... 63-74, 120, 187, 206, 224-225
Revival ... 206, 220-221
Revivalist ... 205
Rice, John R. ... 13, 104, 108, 140
Righteousness ... 93-95
Roberts, Oral ... 223
Robertson, Pat ... 223
Ruler ... 182, 184-186, 195, 198, 202
Ruling ... 180, 184-185
Ryrie, Charles ... 108
Samaritan ... 236-238
Sammis, James ... 121
Samson ... 59
Sanctify ... 59, 116-119, 220
Satan ... 17, 32, 55-56, 92, 95, 153, 155, 212
Saul, King ... 59, 144
Seal ... 47-48, 95, 115
Secular ... 133, 183

Dr. Larry A. Maxwell

Scripture Index
Listed in the Biblical Order

Dr. Larry A. Maxwell

Dr. Larry A. Maxwell

Made in the USA
Middletown, DE
01 August 2017